# THE EARNHARDTS

# THE EARNHARDTS

## A Biography

Gerry Souter

GREENWOOD BIOGRAPHIES

**GREENWOOD PRESS**
*An Imprint of ABC-CLIO, LLC*

A B C 🔻 C L I O

Santa Barbara, California • Denver, Colorado • Oxford, England

**Library of Congress Cataloging-in-Publication Data**
Souter, Gerry.
   The Earnhardts : a biography / Gerry Souter.
      p. cm. — (Greenwood biographies)
   Includes bibliographical references and index.
   ISBN 978-0-313-35840-1 (hard copy : alk. paper) — ISBN 978-0-313-35841-8
(ebook)  1. Earnhardt, Dale, 1951–2001.  2. Earnhardt, Dale, Jr.  3. Stock car
drivers—United States—Biography.  4. Stock car racing—United States.  I. Title.
   GV1032.A1S62  2009
   796.72092'2—dc22
   [B]        2009016127

13  12  11  10  9    1  2  3  4  5

This book is also available on the World Wide Web as an eBook.
Visit www.abc-clio.com for details.

ABC-CLIO, LLC
130 Cremona Drive, P.O. Box 1911
Santa Barbara, California 93116-1911

This book is printed on acid-free paper ∞
Manufactured in the United States of America

If you are in control, you're not going fast enough.

—*Parnelli Jones, race driver*

# CONTENTS

CONTENTS

*Photo essay appears following page 62*

# SERIES FOREWORD

In response to high school and public library needs, Greenwood developed this distinguished series of full-length biographies specifically for student use. Prepared by field experts and professionals, these engaging biographies are tailored for high school students who need challenging yet accessible biographies. Ideal for secondary school assignments, the length, format and subject areas are designed to meet educators' requirements and students' interests.

Greenwood offers an extensive selection of biographies spanning all curriculum-related subject areas including social studies, the sciences, literature and the arts, history and politics, as well as popular culture, covering public figures and famous personalities from all time periods and backgrounds, both historic and contemporary, who have made an impact on American and/or world culture. Greenwood biographies were chosen based on comprehensive feedback from librarians and educators. Consideration was given to both curriculum relevance and inherent interest. The result is an intriguing mix of the well known and the unexpected, the saints and sinners from long-ago history and contemporary pop culture. Readers will find a wide array of subject choices from fascinating crime figures like Al Capone to inspiring pioneers like Margaret Mead, from the greatest minds of our time like Stephen Hawking to the most amazing success stories of our day like J. K. Rowling.

While the emphasis is on fact, not glorification, the books are meant to be fun to read. Each volume provides in-depth information about the subject's life from birth through childhood, the teen years, and adulthood. A thorough account relates family background and education, traces

personal and professional influences, and explores struggles, accomplishments, and contributions. A timeline highlights the most significant life
events against a historical perspective. Bibliographies supplement the ref-
erence value of each volume.

# INTRODUCTION

The announcer's excited voice crackles from speakers mounted high above the grandstands and infield crowd. "Gentlemen, start your engines!" Everyone is standing. The summer North Carolina air is hot and moist. It lies on the skin like a thin film of oil, and salty beads of sweat bubble to the surface. A deep-throated banging sound hangs in the distance: barroom . . . barroom . . . bratta . . . bratta . . . bratta . . . echoing and caroming off the concrete bowl that surrounds the asphalt track, not so much a sound as a jarring of the guts, a rattling of the breeze that thousands suck in and blow out. The anticipation is intoxicating, liberating, as everyone looks into the racetrack's first turn, 30,000 pairs of eyes fixed on one place, on one strip of rubber-smeared asphalt. And the ear-piercing, unmuffled explosions blend into a drumming roar, ever closer. Insects in the grass take flight. The ground shakes; and suddenly, two-abreast, the cars are there.

The cars are plastered against the high-banking, lacquered beetles on rails, pressed by their own momentum into the rubber-grooved road. The roar becomes a guttural shriek, the shriek a howl—cheeyow–chyow–chyow-chyow-chyow—and the howl hammers the eardrums as the rainbow of raw power hurtles past: red-blue-yellow-blue-green-yellow-blue-red-red-black-orange. A vortex of smells—hot oil, gas, rubber, seared iron—swirls in their wake with debris sucked up from the track. An explosion of cheers erupts from 30,000 throats, and the fans who sweated under the Carolina sun release their excitement like a volley of artillery.

The front-runners, the hard-chargers, the pole-sitters, the rookies, the veterans, and the back-markers, helmeted and caged in steel, hurtle between the concrete grandstands and the pits where their crews punch electronic timers and key computers. The drivers aim cars that look like the family cars in the parking lot, stock cars, street cars, the car you drive to work, the car you drive to the store, or the beach, or the zoo. But no car off the dealer's showroom floor ever sounded like that, or hauled coal down the backstretch at 200 miles per hour.

Welcome to American stock car racing.

Three generations of Earnhardts have roared across the start-finish line. This is a story of Ralph Earnhardt, Dale Earnhardt, and Dale Earnhardt Jr.—their heritage and legacy. It is also a story of the rarified world of the National Association for Stock Car Auto Racing (NASCAR), where the Earnhardts, father and son, competed and where their line continues to thrive. The history of the Earnhardts *is* the history of NASCAR. Neither story would be the same without the other. There are as many stories of shoeless backwoods kids growing up to become stock car–racing winners as there are racers on any given track any given day. There are also racing families, fathers and sons who raced with and against each other throughout the history of the sport. Sometimes three brothers ended up in the same race. To race or to watch, stock car racing has always been a family event.

What makes the Earnhardts special is the span of their unique dynasty as winning father handed off to winning son who handed off to his winning son, who competes today. All of them became champions in their eras. There are great winning moments for all three and tragedy for two. Their careers span the life of NASCAR from before its birth in the 1940s to the giant franchise it has become today. There are many winning moments and tragedies within those decades as well. NASCAR's rules governed the Earnhardts' racing lives—both on and off the track. The gaudy, noisy, fan-fueled spectacle of the big 500-mile races of today, where Dale Earnhardt Jr. runs cars and represents his JR Motorsports Company, is a far cry from his grandfather Ralph's dirt-track sprints from the 1940s where the audience left the races digging red clay dust out of their ears. Beginning in the 1970s, Dale Earnhardt inherited his father Ralph's reputation for the hard-charging, take-no-prisoners style of driving that earned Dale championships, cheers, and boos from the fans, and both admiration and curses from fellow drivers. He became an icon that transcended the sport. His name became a brand, an industry, a lifestyle to his fans.

This is the story of how American stock car racing was born and continues today and how an American racing family won, lost, and won again to create three legends in the sport.

# ACKNOWLEDGMENTS

The inventory of literature available on the life of Dale Earnhardt and the history of NASCAR is huge, and I am indebted to the vast number of authors who have documented both the Earnhardt family legacy and the rise of stock car racing in the United States. No one has produced a book that examines the development of Ralph Earnhardt, Dale, and Dale Jr. in the context of their culture—NASCAR and the world of stock car racing—and that is what I have attempted.

Research has included trips to North Carolina to speak with people who knew and grew up with the Earnhardts as well as to visit Kannapolis, Charlotte, Concord, and the Garage Mahal of Dale Earnhardt Inc. (DEI) to walk the grounds. DEI rises at the edge of a two-lane country road like an Inca Temple and reveals the perfect glitzy show business image of NASCAR, hidden behind walls and reflecting the visiting public images in its mirrored façade.

I also interviewed Marshall Brooks, a longtime pal of Dale, as well as Steve Gantt, who led us to other sources. I stood atop Lowe's Speedway in Concord and looked down on Car of Tomorrow tests in the empty track, feeling the power of the machines and observing the shape of race cars to come.

Mr. Norris Dearman curates a collection of Kannapolis, North Carolina, history at the Charles A. Cannon Memorial Library. He threw open his files to me—files reaching back to the days when the textile mills rolled and Ralph Earnhardt raced the local dirt tracks to support his family. Mr. Dearman took me on a tour through town to the Earnhardt home and the statue of Dale in the square, telling stories and pointing out locations little known to tourists and key to the Earnhardt saga.

Interweaving the story of this racing family with the growth of NASCAR reveals two worlds that could not exist without each other. There are many stories like this one that are part of the stock car–racing culture, but the Earnhardts are unique in their consistent trails to victory. They truly are the stuff of legend.

# TIMELINE: EVENTS IN THE LIVES OF THE EARNHARDTS

| | |
|---|---|
| 1920–1932 | Stock car racing gets its start during Prohibition, with moonshine runners attempting to flee federal tax agents. |
| February 23, 1928 | Ralph Lee Earnhardt born in Concord, North Carolina. |
| September 26, 1909 | Bill France Sr. born in Washington, D.C. |
| 1931 | France marries Anne Bledsoe. |
| 1934 | France and Bledsoe drive to Daytona with only a toolbox and $25 to begin work at the Daytona Motor Company. |
| December 14, 1947 | Bill France Sr. holds a meeting in Daytona Beach, Florida, to discuss the future of stock car racing, and NASCAR is conceived. |
| February 15, 1948 | First NASCAR race is run in Daytona at the beach road course. |
| February 21 | NASCAR is incorporated. |
| September 4, 1950 | The Southern 500, NASCAR's first 500-mile race, is held at Darlington Raceway. |
| April 29, 1951 | Dale Earnhardt born. |
| 1954 | NASCAR's first road race, the International 100, is held at Linden Airport in New Jersey. |
| 1956 | Ralph Earnhardt captures the 1956 NASCAR Sportsman championship and wins his first Grand National race—The Buddy Schuman 250, in Hickory, North Carolina. |

| 1958 | Fireball Roberts is voted Professional Athlete of the Year by Florida sportswriters, a first-time award for a race driver. |
|---|---|
| February 22, 1959 | Lee Petty wins the first Daytona 500. |
| July 16, 1961 | ABC Sports televises two hours of the Firecracker 250 from Daytona on *Wide World of Sports*. Ralph Earnhardt finishes Grand National Cup season in 17th Place—best finish. |
| September 13, 1962 | Mamie Reynolds becomes the first female-winning car owner (with Fred Lorenzen driving) at Augusta Speedway in Georgia. |
| December 1, 1963 | Wendell Scott is the first African American to win a premier division NASCAR race at Jacksonville Speedway. |
| 1964 | Richard Petty wins the first of seven championships. |
| 1967 | Dale Earnhardt marries Latane Brown. They are divorced in 1970. |
| September 14, 1969 | Alabama International Speedway—known today as Talladega Superspeedway—opens. |
| December 8 | Dale fathers son, Kerry. |
| 1970 | Dale marries Brenda Lorraine Gee. |
| March 24 | Buddy Baker becomes the first driver to break 200 miles per hour. |
| February 14, 1971 | Motor Racing Network (MRN) broadcasts its first Daytona 500. |
| January 10, 1972 | Bill France Sr. hands leadership of NASCAR to his son, Bill France Jr. |
| August 28 | Dale Earnhardt fathers daughter, Kelley. |
| 1973 | Ralph Earnhardt dies of a heart attack at the age of 45. Won track titles at 11 different speedways in Pennsylvania, Florida, and Tennessee. |
| October 10, 1974 | Dale Earnhardt fathers son, Dale Jr. |
| May 25, 1975 | Dale makes first career Winston Cup start on May 25 at Charlotte Motor Speedway in the World 600. Driving for owner Ed Negre, he starts 33rd and finishes 22nd. |
| 1978 | Jimmy Carter invites NASCAR drivers to the White House. |
| April 1, 1979 | Dale wins Rookie of the Year honors and scores his first career Winston Cup victory at Bristol |

Motor Speedway on April 1, in only his 16th start. Later captures first of 22 career poles.

**November 18**   Richard Petty wins his record seventh series championship.

**1980**   Dale Wins first of seven Winston Cup Championships, becoming the only driver to win Rookie of the Year and championship in back-to-back years.

**1981**   Car owner Rod Osterlund sells team to Jim Stacy. Dale Earnhardt then leaves to drive for Richard Childress.

**1982**   Dale begins first of two seasons driving for Buddy Moore.

Marries Teresa Houston.

**1983**   Scores first of his record 10 wins at Talladega Superspeedway in the DieHard 500.

**1984**   Dale hooks up with car owner Childress again, this time for good.

**1986**   Dale wins second Winston Cup Championship, by winning five races.

NASCAR renames its premier series the NASCAR Winston Cup Series.

**1987**   Statistically, Dale Earnhardt has the most dominating year of his career, recording 11 victories, at one point reeling off 4 in a row. He finishes in the top five 21 times in 29 races and wins third Winston Cup Championship.

**April 30**   Bill Elliott sets fastest speed record at 212.809 miles per hour at Talladega.

**1989**   Every race in the NASCAR Cup Series is televised.

Ralph Earnhardt is inducted into the National Motorsports Press Association's Hall of Fame.

**1990**   Dale Earnhardt wins the first of his three IROC Series Championships, (1990, 1995, 1999). He wins a total of nine races this year, plus wins his fourth Winston Cup Championship (earning a record $3,083,056).

**1991**   Dale wins four races en route to his fifth Winston Cup title.

Dale Jr. begins racing at age 17 in Street Stock Division at Concord, North Carolina Speedway.

**November 15, 1992**   Richard Petty retires after 35 years of racing.

**1993**   Dale Earnhardt wins six races and wins sixth Winston Cup title. Also becomes the first three-time winner of The Winston All-Star Race.

**1994**   Dale ties Richard Petty by winning a record seventh Winston Cup points championship. He also reached $3 million mark in earnings for third time in five years.

**1995**   Dale wins the Brickyard 400, in addition to scoring the first road course victory of his career by taking the checkered flag at Sears Point.

**1996**   Dale wins pole at Watkins Glen road course just two weeks after suffering a broken collar bone and sternum in Talladega wreck.

Dale is first Cup driver to test at Sazuka, Japan, and the third driver to start 500 consecutive Winston Cup races.

Dale Jr. moves up to Busch Grand National Circuit.

**1997**   Dale Sr. is first race car driver to appear on a box of Wheaties cereal despite failing to win a race for the first time in 15 seasons. First driver to reach $30 million in all-time American Motor Sports winnings.

Ralph Earnhardt inducted into International Motorsports Hall of Fame.

**1998**   Dale Sr. wins first Daytona 500 in his 20th start, breaking a 59-race winless streak.

He is the first NASCAR driver to address National Press Club in Washington, D.C.

Dale Sr. finishes 8th in season standings, his 18th top-10 finish in 20 years.

NASCAR celebrates its 50th anniversary.

Dale Jr. wins Busch Championship—first third-generation NASCAR champion. Ralph Earnhardt named one of NASCAR's 50 Greatest Drivers.

**1999**   Dale Sr. wins 73rd career race at Bristol and sweeps both events at Talladega. Wins 10th consecutive Twin 125 qualifying race at Daytona.

| | |
|---|---|
| | At the Coca Cola 600 in Charlotte, Dale Sr. races against Dale Jr. for the first time in a Winston Cup race. |
| November 11 | NASCAR signs partnerships with Fox, NBC, and Turner Sports. |
| 2000 | Dale Sr. wins Winston 500 on October 15 at Talladega Superspeedway for his final career 76th victory. |
| | Dale Jr. wins at Texas in 12th start, Richmond in 16th start. First rookie to win Lowe's Speedway "Winston" All-Star Race. |
| February 18, 2001 | Dale Sr. dies on final turn on final lap of season-opening Daytona 500 at the age of 49. |
| | Dale Jr. wins first Daytona victory five months after Dale Sr.'s death at that track. |
| 2002 | Dale Sr. posthumously named to Motorsports Hall of Fame of America. |
| | Dale Jr. makes *People*'s 50 Most Eligible Bachelors List. |
| June 19, 2003 | NASCAR announces a 10-year deal with primary sponsor Nextel, beginning in 2004. |
| 2004 | Ralph Earnhardt is inducted into the Oceanside Rotary Club of Daytona Beach Stock Car Racing Hall of Fame. |
| | The chase for the NASCAR Nextel Cup is introduced, with the top-10 drivers racing for the championship in the last 10 races of the season. |
| February 15 | Dale Jr. wins Daytona 500-mile race. |
| 2006 | Dale Sr. posthumously elected to the International Motorsports Hall of Fame. |
| | NASCAR expands to Mexico City with a new Busch Series event for 2005. |
| March 25, 2007 | The NASCAR Official Car of Tomorrow debuts at the Nextel Cup Food City 500 in Bristol, Tennessee. |
| May | Dale Jr. announces that he will leave Dale Earnhardt Inc. at the end of 2007. |
| June 7 | Bill France Jr. dies at the age of 74. |
| 2008 | Dale Jr. leaves Dale Earnhardt Inc. to join the Hendricks Racing Team. |

**June 15**                Dale Jr. has first win for Hendricks in Michigan.
                           It is his first win in 76 starts, but he runs out of
                           gas as car crosses the finish line. He has to be
                           pushed into victory lane.

**February 9, 2008**       Dale Jr. dominates the Budweiser Shootout sprint
                           at the Daytona Speedway for his first victory driv-
                           ing for the Hendricks Racing Team.

**February 14**            Dale Jr. wins the 150-mile Gatorade Duel, a pre-
                           liminary race to the Daytona 500 at that speed-
                           way.
                           Dale Jr. finishes the 2008 season in third position
                           in the NASCAR points standings after a series of
                           top five and top 10 finishes.

**February 15, 2009**      Dale Jr., down one lap, is involved in a 10 car
                           pile-up at the season-opening 51st running of the
                           Daytona 500.

# Chapter 1

# THE BEGINNING

Today's American stock car racing ballooned from post–World War II dirt tracks where prewar Detroit automobiles coughed out the last of their lives gouging out ruts in red clay to reach the checkered flag of victory. Virtually all civilian automobile production had stopped for the duration of the war so the manufacturers could build tanks, trucks, and airplanes to combat the German and Japanese armies. So in the late 1940s, young men climbed into pre-1940 coupes and sedans with taped-over headlights and well-worn tires. They didn't use seat belts because they feared being trapped in a burning car more than crashing into the wall or other cars. There were no crush-proof helmets or fireproof uniforms—only a baseball cap or soft leather aviator's helmet to keep oil and dirt out of the driver's hair and a pair of goggles to protect the eyes from flying stones. Instead of wearing special racing shoes, they stamped their leather work boots on the gas and clutch pedals and took off down the straightaway until they won, crashed, or were beaten by someone who was faster—or a driver who had better luck that day.

There is no way to understand what made the Earnhardts' impact on American sporting culture stand out so large unless you start in the garage with engine grease under the fingernails and finish on the winner's podium at the end of the race spraying champagne on the cheering crowd. The key to the puzzle is NASCAR. It was created by a handful of those race car drivers and owners in December 1947. They were a hearty, independent collection of self-made good old boys who ate dust and endured overheated engines, the chill of defeat, and the thrill of bringing home the prize purse. Some had spent time in jail for transporting illegal home-brewed whiskey (moonshine) over southern back roads at night and then drove their cars to the race. If they wrecked, they hitched a ride home in the tow truck. Some still carried bullet and shrapnel wounds from World War II, or even deeper pains that made them casual with their lives. Racing stock cars was a tonic, a cure, a job, or an obsession. For some, the winning purse put food on the table and shoes on the kids, which made every race a pressure cooker to avoid facing their families with empty pockets at the end of the day.

The roots of stock car racing in the southern United States are deep in the distilling, transporting, and selling of illegal whiskey cooked in family-owned stills hidden and operated in the deep woods. Whiskey production dated back to pre-Revolutionary times when the Scotch-Irish ancestors of the families who live there today brought distilling skills with them from Scotland and Ireland. Making whiskey was part of the culture in the Appalachian Mountains, the Smokies of Tennessee, and throughout the Carolinas, Georgia, and Virginia. At one time, George Washington operated the largest distillery of spirits in the United States, turning out 11,000 gallons in 1799 from his Mount Vernon estate. The problem arose when the states and federal government taxed whiskey to bring in revenue for new roads, schools, and other modern improvements.

Much of the country where whiskey was made offered few ways to earn a living other than growing corn in small fields amid the rocks, trees, and thick clay soil. Because of small patches of usable land, livestock were raised for family use or barter as were vegetables and tobacco crops. Turning corn into whiskey provided more cash in the pocket for an extended family living close to the poverty line than selling the small crop yields on the market for food and forage. Whole families defied the law and went into the distilling business.

In 1919, when Prohibition—the 18th Amendment to the Constitution called the Volstead Act—made drinking or making whiskey illegal in the United States, federal agents moved hard against the mountain families who made corn whiskey moonshine. The feds could smell corn mash cooking in the pine tree air and see where smoke rose above the woods if some fool let green wood soaked with sap get into the fire under the boilers.

Cooking up a batch of moonshine was a simple recipe. Corn kernels were soaked in water until they sprouted; then they were dried and ground into a malt. The malt was soaked until the corn's starch turned to sugar, or sweet mash, which was mixed with water, sugar, and other crops for flavor, then cooked and stirred until the sugary sludge the thickness of oatmeal turned into alcohol. The waste sludge rose to the top when stirred and was skimmed off, and the remaining alcohol was poured into a pot still and boiled over a wood fire. The alcohol turned into a vapor when boiled at 176 degrees; this vapor found its way up a coiled copper tube called the worm, which passed through a condenser of cool water returning the vapor to a liquid, which dripped into a pail. The first batch, heads, and the last batch of a run, tails, were dumped out as toxic and only the middlings were bottled in screw-top Mason jars for sale as Tiger Spit, White Dog, or Corn Squeezin's. Further west, the clear liquor was often colored with caramel or sometimes dyed reddish brown with a drop or two of iodine and called Busthead or Who-Hit-John. Considerable skill was required to produce clean batches that didn't poison or blind drinkers of the 150-proof whiskey.[1]

The illegal distillers' profits rapidly increased by delivering the raw moonshine to distributors in the larger southern cities using Henry Ford's new mass-produced, affordable automobiles, beginning with the Model T. Deliveries were made more quickly with shorter turnaround times so more batches were cooked. The law, of course, countered with its own flying squads of sheriffs and federal officers in fast cars pursuing or heading off the autos filled to capacity with moonshine. The back roads of the Moonshine States became virtual racetracks as the wily "whiskey trippers" used every trick they could imagine to foil the law.

Even after the Volstead Act was repealed in 1932, taxing of whiskey continued, and by then the creation of vehicles for transporting illegal alcohol had become a cottage industry practiced by "shade tree" mechanics and auto garage owners throughout the South. Anywhere a man handy with tools could toss a block and tackle over the branch of a chinaberry tree became an open-air garage and hang-out for young men with a hankering for speed. The family car often was a Ford coupe with an impractical small cockpit for a large family. It had a new Ford V-8 engine with a higher top speed, extra carburetors attached for greater fuel flow, heavier suspension for cornering on dirt roads, and wide, heavy tires for traction and to eliminate flats. The rear seat could be removed to store cartons of whiskey jars—wrapped to keep them from jingling against each other—or large stainless steel cans of bulk whiskey.

Loaded with gasoline, crammed with gallons of 150 proof 75 percent alcohol, these potential bombs hurtled through the night over unlit dirt roads. For example, in 1934, a million gallons a year of moonshine—from the nationwide total of 35 million gallons—roared down the roads between Dawsonville and Atlanta, Georgia, at a profit of $20 a gallon. Their drivers mashed the gas pedal, one hand on the steering wheel and the other on the gear shift with a Bugle Boy hand-rolled cigarette hanging from their lips. At the end of a week's whiskey trips with a $1,000 in his pocket, a driver could buy himself an even faster car.[2] The trippers were worshipped as heroes in the hills, but often paid a hurtful price for their occupation.

Some died in flaming fireballs after losing control of their rocketing machines; others were crippled and some were hijacked by rival "bootleggers," an antique term for 18th-century traders who carried half-pint flasks of liquor in their riding boots to illegally trade with the Indians. The drivers were robbed of their cargo and often beaten or left dead at the side of the road. Others were trapped in police roadblocks and spent two to three years of their young lives in a state prison working on chain gangs with hardened convicts.

NASCAR doesn't talk about this part of its history, but if racing cars on tracks for prize money and pride accomplished nothing else, it saved a lot of young lives behind the wheels of fast cars—lives which otherwise faced death or prison.

As was natural with high-spirited young men jacked up with adrenaline after a week's worth of dodging the law and with pockets full of cash, a contest seemed in order to see who had the fastest ride. Across the southern states, cow pastures were invaded and bulldozers secured to carve racetracks out of the rocky clay soil. At first, these oval tracks were just used by the trippers who would ante up cash in a coffee can and race for the winnings. But there were smart men around who saw that people in nearby towns flocked to these weekend contests. No way anyone could keep them secret with the roaring engines and rising dust clouds visible for miles. An investment of a little lumber, a few hand-drawn signs, and some sweat equity created a racetrack. Folks who always had some set-aside money hidden away for special occasions found 50 cents to sit in a makeshift grandstand for a few thrills on a Saturday night.

Every driver paid an entry fee for each race and with admission dollars coming in, the final winner of a series of elimination heats could take home $200—enough to feed a family in the 1930s for three weeks and pay off some of the mortgage. The 2nd-place driver might win a box of nickel cigars or a can of motor oil. When it was over, drivers got in their race cars and drove home.

Sometimes these affairs were put together by a couple of fellows—promoters—who got everyone to donate time and labor and when the race was over and the racers came looking for their prize money, the coffee can was empty and the promoters were nowhere to be found.[3] These same crooks headed for another remote county or valley in another state and worked their scheme all over again. Eventually, as telephone lines were strung and communications improved, the fly-by-night race promoters were tracked down. But the racetrack just outside town became a fixture of southern culture.

Promoters of the races were not necessarily the track owners. Anyone with money to risk on drawing a large crowd and to pay the winning drivers a portion of the ticket sales—about 40 percent—could rent the track and advertise the event. Determining a champion of a series of races became a nebulous affair because the series had to be sanctioned by some organization that made the rules for all the races and put up the trophy and tallied the points needed to win. Using a points total, a driver who was consistently 2nd or 3rd in a number of races could become champion without winning a single race.

Rules began separating different kinds of cars into different races. "Stock car" had a vague meaning to racers considering the number of modifications that could be made which were not immediately apparent to a casual observer. Family sedans that brought home the groceries and took the kids to school could end up banging fenders and firing rooster tails of dirt high over the sharp turns in a weekend race. Their entry numbers were painted on the doors over showroom black, green, and maroon body work with water-based paint to be hosed off after the race. Drivers fitted extra-heavy-duty bumpers, a mesh screen, or iron cross-braces to protect the radiator. Hoods over the engine block were removed for quick access and ventilation while the wheels were often unprotected by fenders.

Shade tree mechanics in backwoods garages could work magic on a stock engine, drilling a hole here to allow more air into the carburetor, shaving weight off the chassis, or adding more space for gasoline to keep pit stops for fuel to a minimum. These men were in constant demand by racers and car owners, who might field two or three cars in a race driven by a stable of drivers.

Louis Jerome "Red" Vogt was a legend among mechanics who had a gift for getting maximum speed from a car, but he had virtually no social skills dealing with either his family or the men who hired him. Red Vogt was born in 1904 and started work as a mechanic in a Cadillac agency at age 12. The freckled-face kid immediately showed his abilities and by age 16 was boss of the shop. An early friend was young Bill France who worked as a mechanic in a Ford agency. Together they spent their weekends hunting for races. France borrowed his father's Model T and Vogt straddled a motorcycle for racing on wooden board tracks in Maryland, Pennsylvania, and New Jersey.

After one particularly bad crash from which he carried splinters in his body for the rest of his life, Vogt decided he made more money with a wrench than on a racetrack. He hired himself out to prominent bootleggers to speed up their Fords and filled his pockets with whiskey money. In his own garage, he built a secret room in the rear where he worked on whiskey-car engines in a pristine setting. He had little formal education but his new wife, Ruth, kept his finances straight, and he became quite wealthy in the mid-1930s when the Great Depression was at its peak. His ability to trim weight and add horsepower to a stock car kept him employed, but his personality kept him virtually friendless. He was brutal with his family and had a violent temper with little provocation. His few close friends winced when they saw him abuse his kids, but they swallowed their anger because Red Vogt knew speed.[4] Race car owners began drifting into his shop looking for an edge on the track. He was eager to oblige.

There were sprint cars, which ran on short half-mile-long tracks in elimination heats, and there were long-haul racers, which ran in big 100-mile races that went round and round until the mileage was covered and the winner crossed the start-finish line. The trouble was every sanctioning authority had different rules and winning a race sponsored by one organization didn't count in one's annual tally of wins racing for a different organization. There was money to be earned, but the machinations required to keep everything straight were mind-boggling.

These authorities included: the National Championship Stock Car Circuit, National Stock Car Racing Association, New England Stock Car Circuit, National Auto Racing League, American Automobile Association, South Carolina Racing Association, Sports Car Club of America, Stock Car Auto Racing Society, and others with each one looking to be dominant. The American Automobile Association (AAA) was a venerable organization with a racing wing, the Contest Board, which sanctioned custom open-wheel races such as the Indianapolis 500. For a while, the AAA also tallied numbers and kept track of a few reasonably legitimate stock car races. By 1946, the AAA let the racing community know that it would no longer have anything to do with stock cars—or what they called junk cars. That's when the other authorities blossomed and began elbowing their way into the growing number of weekend events.

Rising to the top of this chaos was the National Stock Car Racing Association (NSRA) based in Atlanta, the National Championship Stock Car Racing Association (NCSRA), and the National Championship Stock Car Circuit (NCSCC) run by Bill France. The good mechanic and boyhood pal of Red Vogt grew up into a tall and rangy adult with a gift for promotion. France was born on September 26, 1909, in Washington, D.C., and settled into working on cars in Ford dealerships until he built his first race car in 1926 and began dirt-track racing on short tracks around his hometown. He married his wife, Anne Bledsoe, in 1931, and in 1934 they headed south to a warmer climate. They got as far as the beach community of Daytona, Florida, where, with only his toolbox and $25, France started work at the Daytona Motor Company to earn a living.

By 1935, Daytona suddenly found itself without its main claim to fame. Land-speed record breakers had used its flat hard beach to make their runs to beat the clock. On March 7, 1935, Malcolm Campbell took his custom-built Bluebird V racer to 276 miles per hour over a measured mile. Soon after that hot run, other record-seeking racers discovered the Bonneville Salt Flats in Utah, and Daytona deflated to become another wide space in the road. Daytona businesses needed to keep the town's reputation for speed alive to survive. They did this by using a straight section of Highway A1A, carving out a parallel section of the beach, and adding a curve at each end to form an oval, part-sand and part-macadam racetrack. Bill France set aside his tools and entered the first race. He came in 5th, beginning his driving career that extended into 1950.

While still racing in 1946, France promoted some stock car races and he came up with the idea for a 100-mile race to be run in Charlotte, North Carolina, with the winner being proclaimed a champion. Unfortunately, that title would not be honored by the press without the race being sanctioned by a recognized racing authority. Instead of seeking out an authority, France created his own, the National Championship Stock Car Circuit (NCSCC) which sponsored a number of races through 1947. By the end of that year, Bill France had shaped in his mind the kind of overall umbrella organization that would govern the entire stock car-racing community. His brainchild would establish rules for cars and licensing drivers, tally win points, approve track safety, sanction races, award championships, build a media presence in the press and, most of all, make money, big money for all concerned.

In the fall of 1947, Bill France met in the Hotel Wilkes in North Wilkesboro, North Carolina, with a few of the pioneer racetrack promoters. They included Enoch Staley and Paul Sawyer of the Richmond Fairgrounds Raceway, as well as Alvin Hawkins from the Darlington Raceway, Clay Earles representing the Speedway at Martinsville, and Joe Little John up from Spartanburg, South Carolina. With meetings like this, involving those promoters who had the biggest stake in a successful racing franchise and organization, France laid the groundwork for his biggest leap of all, turning southern-style stock car–racing into a respectable, money-making sport.[5]

When he was ready, Bill France moved fast. Over three days, December 14–17, 1947, France gathered together 35 representatives from all parts of the racing community to the Ebony Room of Daytona's art deco

Streamline Hotel. With tables pushed together in a conference room, this meeting hammered out the structure of the new venture that would be called the National Association for Stock Car Auto Racing (NA-SCAR).

These young racers, older veterans, car owners, whiskey trippers, and car dealers needed to guarantee winning money, set up a system of points to race for, and proclaim a champion when the year ran out. They needed to set standards for the cars. What kind of cars could race each other? Where could they race and what safety standards could keep drivers alive when the racetrack bit them? There was not a whole lot of formal education in that hotel room, but those present were serious about their sport and saw an opportunity to make something that would last from a scattered collection of ideas. Throughout the southern United States, there was a huge audience from which to build a fan base and leapfrog into America's most popular spectator sport with magnitudes of growth the men in that hotel room never imagined.

## NOTES

1. Neal Thompson, *Driving with the Devil* (New York: Crown Publishers, 2006), pp. 20–21.

2. Ibid., p. 60.

3. Peter Golenbock, *NASCAR Confidential* (St. Paul, MN: MBI Publishing, 2004), pp. 45–47.

4. Thompson, pp. 73–76.

5. Andrew J. Baker, When the Engines No Longer *Roar: A Case Study of North Wilkesboro, NC and the North Wilkesboro Speedway*, 2005, http://www.savethe speedway.net/history1.html.

# Chapter 2

# NASCAR STARTS CUTTING ITS TEETH

Racetracks had already become big business by the time NASCAR began adding its official stamp to the contests. For example, the speedway at North Wilkesboro, North Carolina, was a going concern in May 1946. An oval 5/8 of a mile (.625) had been carved out of the clay, but with only a $1,500 budget for the entire project, the grading was cut short leaving the front stretch running downhill, forcing the drivers to climb uphill on the backstretch. Its unofficial race was a contest scrambled together by some local whiskey trippers.

Every track had its local legend and the top-dog driver everyone wanted to beat. In North Wilkesboro, that driver became Robert Glenn "Junior" Johnson. He lived only 10 miles outside town and one day he was standing in a cornfield, shouldering a single-bottom plow and staring at the south end of a north-bound mule when he heard his name called from the roadway.

"I was 16, plowing a mule and planting corn for my father when my older brother L. P. drove up to the field and said they were going to have a race over at the new North Wilkesboro Speedway. He wanted me to drive his liquor car, a 1940 Ford. All the cars racing at North Wilkesboro then were liquor cars."[1]

About 20 cars showed up for that race, all 1939 and 1940 sedans with hopped-up engines and stripped-out interiors. The race itself was a crude affair driven with more enthusiasm than skill as the big, clunky Fords, Plymouths, and Buicks skidded and scuffed through potholes and places where the grading hadn't been finished. Drivers jounced around, thumping their sculls on the headers, and grounded their oil pans as suspensions heaved the chassis from hole to hole. Junior Johnson went on to both local and national fame with 50 NASCAR wins and enough cash to build his own chicken ranch.

But the North Wilkesboro Speedway opened officially on that May afternoon in 1946 to grandstands seating 3,000 locals. By final count, at least 10,000 paying customers streamed in. It was a story taking place all through the South. Young men put down their tools at the furniture factory, the hosiery factory, or the other mills and factories where cheap Appalachian labor did the handwork and went home to lift the hood of the family sedan and think about going racing. The life seemed uncertain and families needed steady paychecks.

NASCAR, under the ambitious drive of Bill France and a growing group of backers and racers, took the junk car meets in cow-pasture tracks and turned them into crowd-pleasing spectacles with winning purses that were worth the risk—racetracks that had bloomed like mushrooms on a log all over the South and up into the Midwest. Even far-off California offered legitimate sanctioned venues for championship stock car racing.

The beauty of NASCAR racing was there were race classes for everyone during this start-up time. The majority of tracks were crude affairs, carved out of a field with a road grader and bulldozer, ringed in with chicken wire fencing and following the same patterns of an oval with at least two straight runs and four corners. Most were a mile or less in length. In the center of the oval, a long hole was scooped out of the red clay earth to store extra tires and gas cans. It was called the Pit and to get to it off the racing surface, the driver turned into the center of the oval onto the Pit Road that paralleled the straight that ran past the cobbled-together, uncovered grandstands.

The sanctioned cars—those approved by the NASCAR rules and inspectors—were classified into divisions as Strictly Stock, Modified Stock, Sportsman, and two short-lived, but popular divisions: Speedway for open-wheel racers like the custom-built racing machines that ran at the Indianapolis 500 each year and Convertibles. These chop-tops ran together as a class because they weren't fast enough to compete with the enclosed cars and their lighter chopped frames. The word "stock" came to mean whatever race-improved version of the car was allowed on the track. NASCAR 1948 rules stated:

- Foreign manufactured cars will not be permitted.
- Stock bumpers and mufflers must be removed (too fragile).
- Cars must be equipped with a rearview mirror.
- Cars can be run with or without fan or generator.

Though the outside shell was a Ford, Chevrolet, Oldsmobile, Hudson, Nash or Plymouth, the motor, drive-train gears, tires, and suspension were often anything but stock. The divisions were designed to allow racing modifications up to a point so that all the cars in a race were competitive. The strictly stock cars drew the best crowds and most approval from spectators resembling as they did the cars that could be bought off dealers' lots. But some mechanics or "wrenches"—like Red Vogt—were a bit sharper than others when it came to squeezing speed out of a stock car.

The first strictly stock NASCAR race promoted by Bill France was run in June 1949 in Charlotte, North Carolina, to cover 150 miles for a $5,000 purse. Until that time, the biggest draws had been to modified car races where considerable changes were allowed, pretty much stripping the identity of the vehicle down to its remaining cockpit. Automobile brand loyalty had grown into definite camps. There were Ford men and Plymouth supporters. Big Buicks had a fan base as did Chevrolet, Nash, and Hudson. And on June 19, 1949, when the flag dropped and the field came snorting down that Charlotte racetrack, the charge of Detroit iron looked like Sunday traffic gone mad. Where old jalopies had once clanked and clattered around the clay in junk car races for years, new cars like the ones the tourists drove through town, or the cars that belonged to folks who drove to church and lived higher on the hog than most of the audience; now, these showroom beauties traded door licks, fender tags, and bumper shoves burrowing down into that first rutted turn.

Engines overheated; tires blew with a "Pow! Phweeee!"; and drivers hung on to their oversize steering wheels, shoulders against the door, steering cockeyed, scuttling sideways like crabs on three wheels and one rim to make it back to the pits for new rubber. Pressure from high- speed turns warped regular driving tires right off their rims, so the rules allowed drivers to reinforce their wheels with steel plates to keep the rubber in place. Tape covered headlights to keep broken glass from littering the track. Fan blades snapped off their whirring hubs, carved through sheet metal hoods, spun whistling through the air, and buried their knife edges in the track's woodwork like hurled machetes. Radiators exploded, firing hot water and steam-geysering into the air followed by black smoke of cooking oil and sparks of searing iron. Around and around they went. One driver arrived late and found he had no car to drive. He talked a couple into borrowing their new Oldsmobile 88. After taping all the chrome and headlights, he drove the race, coming in 5th—and only smashed up the front end a little bit.

In the end, Hubert Westmoreland crossed the finish line 1st in a Ford followed three laps back by Jim Roper, who had driven his 1949 Lincoln from Kansas to arrive in time for the race. Following the race, however—and this would become a nagging feature of NASCAR racing—it was found that Westmoreland's Ford was a modified whiskey tripper with beefed-up rear springs. That made Jim Roper winner of the first NAS-CAR-sanctioned strictly stock car race—which he found out the following day.

Other racers who finished out of the money pried fenders straight enough to keep from cutting tires and either rolled their scraped and dented autos onto a flatbed trailer or gassed up for the long drive home. Some drove back to towns where they had jobs or to farms where they worked the land. Others drove to homes where they had a garage out back and just enough money in the cookie jar—after buying the week's groceries and putting something on the mortgage payment—to replace a punctured radiator or invest in a new clutch and get ready for the next race down the road.

## NOTE

1. Andrew J. Baker, When the Engines No Longer *Roar: A Case Study of North Wilkesboro, NC and the North Wilkesboro Speedway*, 2005, http://www.savethe speedway.net/history1.html.

# Chapter 3

# THE LEGACY BEGINS

Ralph Lee Earnhardt was one of those, a full-time race driver.

Tall, rangy, all elbows and knees, Ralph Lee Earnhardt was a quiet man, born on February 23, 1928, in Kannapolis, North Carolina, just outside of Charlotte to his parents, Effie May Barber and John Henderson Earnhardt. He was raised during the Great Depression and accustomed to a level of poverty as were his neighbors in the small town. Ralph and his wife, Martha, had five children born between 1948 and 1955. Being a responsible family man, Ralph went to work in the nearby Cannon textile mill—Kannapolis means City of Looms in Greek—and joined the ranks of the "Lintheads," who labored amid the airborne lint fibers and constant mist of oil from the whirring bobbins that stored raw fiber as thread, the vibrating wood floors, and the heavy lifting. But mostly he liked to take apart and put together automobiles.

Good mechanics were abundant in the South where the Depression had hit hard and learning how to repair motors and mechanical gadgets saved money that could be put to better use. Ralph had a gift for building race cars out of junkyard parts and when he found that he enjoyed testing his creations as much as building them, he began to race other drivers on dirt tracks for bragging rights. In many small towns that were little more than a general store and a gas station, the quiet man patiently waiting in line to buy a sack of potatoes became a hard-charging, competitive driver rooster-tailing around dirt-track curves on weekends.

Finally, Ralph could not haul his lunch bucket back to that lint factory one more day. He quit his mill job to go stock car racing for cash full-time. This was a terribly risky commitment to make for a family man who grew up during the Depression when just having *any* job was a survival skill. The earlier generation of young men scattered throughout the hill country of the Appalachian Mountains had risked jail for the money they earned driving high-speed cars running illegal whisky from back-country stills to city bootleggers. Ralph Earnhardt bet everything on his ability to build fast cars and win races rather than risk jail time with a family to support.

His wife, Martha, said later, "When he first told me he was going to quit his job and race, I thought, 'Well, he's lost his mind.' I threatened to leave him, but he just kept talking. He promised me that if he couldn't do it without taking away from the family, he would quit. He always kept me and the five kids up without me having to work, so I couldn't say too much."[1]

He embarked on a series of races on small dirt tracks around his home, risking entry-fee money each time and needing to win to more than break even. Most dirt tracks offered about $150 to the winner. If he crashed, he couldn't race until the car was repaired. Over time, the wins outpaced the losses and Ralph learned to drive with great consistency, not straining his car and remaining always near the front of the melee churning through the red clay ruts. When he wasn't racing, Ralph spent time combing through junkyards for parts.

He could take a 1939 Ford with a teardrop hood, put an oversize Lincoln radiator in front of the engine, stuff some asbestos between the radiator and the hood, and tie the whole package in place with rope. Working like that he could create a modified stock race car for about $800. If he wrecked it in a race, he would salvage what he could from the engine and drive train and buy another body from the junkyard for $50. Anything else he needed was usually available from the same junkyard buffet. As for safety, Earnhardt wore an old midget racer helmet and tied a homemade leather belt across his lap. He also wore a pair of leather gloves to prevent blisters and favored slacks and a T-shirt to drive in the North Carolina heat and a button-up coverall when the air turned chilly.[2]

In the 1950s, race drivers paid considerable attention to their tires, and drivers like Ralph earned money testing tires under race conditions. Race promoters like veteran Howard Wheeler Jr.—called Humpy by his friends, learned to trust Earnhardt, his common working-class civility, and the way he raced his car. He was Wheeler's chief southern, weekly dirt-track tester during the time Wheeler worked for Firestone Tire & Rubber Company.

Tires have always been an expensive item for racers, who often go through many sets during a race or series of elimination heats. Tire companies learned that racers were good testers for rubber compounds and tread designs that found their way onto family autos. Winning races was also good advertising for the tire manufacturers. Ralph Earnhardt ran on a particularly demanding surface, gritty abrasive clay that scoured the tire's surface causing the treads to lose traction and threatened sidewalls with blowouts. The tires flexed and distorted with the almost continual four-wheel drifts—where the front wheels remain pointed at the center of the track while the rear wheels push the rear end toward the right side rail—required to negotiate the tight turns without losing speed. Many of the tracks once ran small wheelbase midget cars so the radius of each turn was small and the turns were close together in the short distance from start to checkered flag. For the larger NASCAR Modified and Modified Sportsman Division stock cars, the drivers were almost always turning left, grinding away at the narrow tires of the period.

Ralph Earnhardt helped pioneer the concept of tire stagger to take advantage of the constant left-turning dirt tracks. As the car drives into the turn, the outside wheels are pushing the car to the left. The inside wheels should not fight this force, so the tire size of the inside rear (power) wheel is slightly smaller because it is traveling a relatively shorter distance. This reduced travel causes a drag on the inside, which pushes the front of the car to the left. This system works when a car has no differential to control the speed of outside and inside split axels that maximize turning performance on a paved track. The solid rear axels that Earnhardt used work best on loose dirt tracks that allow the car to slide through turns.[3]

Earnhardt's ability to alter his tire stagger to match the track, or give "bite" into the turns, gave him an edge in every race. Sometimes he raced five times a week, slamming through the pack of both good and amateur drivers who could put up the entry fee. He earned two nicknames. One was Mr. Consistency for his ability to keep his car near the front and be patient while the hard chargers burned out their cars or crashed. There's a fine line between keeping a car in contention and stroking or sandbagging—driving conservatively to stay out of trouble.[4] He was banned from a track in Hickory, North Carolina, for winning too many races. Attendance dropped when he was entered and the track lost money.

Ralph Earnhardt always drove to win. He told Dale early on, "There's only one lap you need to lead, and that's the last lap."[5]

His other nickname was Ironheart for his sheer endurance, showing up night after night, maybe having a couple of pals help him unload the car from the trailer and pitch in gassing or changing tires in the pits as needed. Driving those big Sportsman and Modified sedans of the '40s and '50s, stripped of everything nonessential to winning the race was hard work. Suspensions and springs were tight. Every pebble in the dirt track, every scuff of a tire against the rail or an opponent, every shunt from the front or rear traveled right through the bare cockpit, up the steering wheel, and hammered the arms and legs. Red dirt blew in where the side windows had been and at the end of the race, every driver wore a sheen of clay and sweat on his bare arms and face and had dirt ground into the creases of his pants and shirts. They inhaled dirt, spit dirt, and washed dirt from their mouths with a swig of water, soda pop, or something stronger. Like coal miners, dirt racers take part of the track home with them that no amount of scrubbing can every completely remove.

At the end of each race, he ran his battered Modified or Sportsman racer onto a trailer and towed it home to get the car ready for the next competition. Racing was a nine-to-five job divided between garage work building the cars and fixing what broke and the hours spent skidding and jouncing behind a roaring unmuffled engine amid the stink of gasoline, tortured rubber, and shearing metal. Earnhardt built crash bars into the doors of his cars to make the metal cockpit walls even more rigid in case of a rollover. His seat belt was also an uncommon accessory in the 1940s, but driving wasn't a hobby, or pastime; Earnhardt was a breadwinner. He couldn't afford to be sick or injured. There was no health care insurance, no pension plan, and no guaranteed employment. He applied for a new job as a winning race driver every week, but gradually assembled a resume that earned him a spot at the start of any race he chose to enter.

According to Ned Jarrett, another NASCAR winner, "Ralph Earnhardt was absolutely the toughest race driver I ever raced against. On the dirt and asphalt short tracks in Sportsman competition you went to the track you knew he was the man to beat."[6]

Earnhardt's racing style in those early days was hardly that of a wild man like Junior Johnson, who drove the wheels off his rides and took no prisoners out there on the track. In the 1940s before certifications, races were driven by young men with a broad range of experience. This meant anyone who could pony up the entry fee could be a member of the club when the green start flag dropped. After passing a cursory car inspection, the driver simply pushed his car to the start line and maybe had a couple of friends in the pits to help with gas and tire-changing chores as the contest wore on.

Every race had a clutch of eager rookies salted among the seasoned veterans, those who had brought home winnings and those who were winless but had the fever. Earnhardt told his son Dale when the boy started racing, "Establish your territory."[7] And that's how Ralph drove, settling in to 2nd or 3rd place as the laps wound down. He guarded that position, staying close to the front, but letting the hard chargers mash down the gas pedal until they wrecked kiting into a turn, burned up a wheel bearing, blew a radiator hose, or suffered any of the many race-ending catastrophes. Then he moved.

A stock car race in those days sounded like one long collision. When someone moved, pushing his car through a hole between two other cars to pass them both, often, that hole closed. When he drove for groceries and the mortgage payment, lifting off the gas was not an option as the laps dwindled. Ralph Earnhardt swapped paint and pushed his fenders forward hunting for clear air at the front of the pack. Most of the time he had one of the better-prepared cars running, but it also had to run next week and the weekend after that. The car was his place of business. He might have pushed his ride out front earlier and won by a couple of laps, but those Modified race cars cobbled together of scavenged parts had limited durability and could only be pushed so far.

Young Dale would often get out of bed early after his father returned from racing and cross the yard to the garage where Ralph parked and worked on his race cars. Still plastered with the red clay from its last race, the racer told its story. "All I had to do was look at the front end," said Dale. "If the front end was pretty clean that meant he had a good race and probably won."[8]

Ralph Earnhardt built his Modified cars from the ground up. He made them strong where they needed to be strong. Besides creating one of the first roll cages of tubing to protect the driver in a rollover crash, he also shaved away metal wherever possible. Rear-wheel fenders came off his Go or Blow coupe. The front fenders were minimized to flaps cut out high to keep mud from hitting the windscreen, but leaving the tires wide open for fast changing. The hood was shaved, covering just the top of the engine compartment and leaving the sides open for ventilation. He reinforced the vulnerable radiator because there were no recognizable bumpers up front. The 1940s Modified race cars built for the dirt tracks made no pretensions of being family sedans. They were built to race and shave what rules there were in force at the time to the ragged edge. Ingenuity had to take the place of dollars when it came to problem solving. A story circulates through NASCAR history of a rule change that caused the soft steel axel keys to break on many cars. Ralph discovered the diameter of a Number Six screwdriver matched the key and the driver shaft was higher quality tempered steel. He then proceeded to buy up just about every Number Six screwdriver in the state of North Carolina.

Unlike today's advertising decal-emblazoned stock cars, sponsors were few in the days when Ralph raced. They had yet to realize the power of those colorful patches, slogans, and corporate logos plastered to cars circling past thousands of fans again and again. Each race, there were only a few dollars added to the pot, which was mostly dependent on hand-lettered names and addresses of mom-and-pop stores, garages, or local companies such as Ralph's main sponsor, Dainty Maid Food Products.

Back at the Sedan Street garage behind his house in Kannapolis, he'd hand the lug wrench to his partner to work on the wheel nuts. The little boy who knelt by the scuffed and torn rubber was Ralph Dale Earnhardt born in 1951 and virtually lived in Ralph Lee Earnhardt's shadow whenever there was car work to be done. While he made himself as useful as his years permitted, NASCAR began to shape the sport and consolidate the fractured and scattered tracks, rules, and car classes into a commercial success.

## NOTES

1. Kenny Mane, *The Dale Earnhardt Story* (New York: Hyperion, 2004), p. 21.

2. Joe Menzer, *The Wildest Ride: A History of NASCAR* (New York: Simon & Schuster, 2001), pp. 122–123.

3. Team Associated, "Handling vs. Cornering Power," www.teamassociated.com/racerhub/techhelp/marc/Handling.6.html.

4. AutoSpeak, "Dictionary of Racing Terms," http://www.autospeak.com/terms99.htm.

5. Mane, p. 23.

6. Tom Gillispie, *I Remember Dale Earnhardt* (Nashville, TN: Cumberland House, 2001), p. 54.

7. Ibid., p. 117.

8. Mane, p. 21.

# Chapter 4

# NASCAR—THROUGH THE 1950s

Two events marked the maturing NASCAR as it said good-by to the 1940s. At the end of 1948 and a schedule of 52 dirt-track races, Bill France Sr. awarded the first winning checks to drivers who earned the most points during that inaugural year. The points system—which awarded points for drivers finishing 1st, 2nd, and 3rd—was worked out earlier on a bar napkin. Second place went to Fonty Flock for $600 ($5,317 in modern dollars) and $1,200 ($10,635 in modern dollars) to Robert "Red" Byron for 1st place.

Byron was both typical for the race drivers of that period and exceptional for sheer determination. Born in 1915, he flew B-24 Liberator bombers from the Aleutian Islands in World War II. He was shot down by enemy fire and required surgery that crippled his left leg. After two years of hospitalization, he went racing with reduced mobility of that leg. Byron created a harness that strapped his foot to the car's clutch. Even with this handicap he managed to win NASCAR's 1948 Modified championship over Marshall Teague and drove Oldsmobiles for car owner Raymond Parks to win the 1949 title in what later became the NASCAR Winston Cup Series.

Byron was a racer in the same mold as Ralph Earnhardt, taking his time, staying close to the leaders, saving his car until near the end of the race and then coming on hard, tooling through the pack with a chomped cigar in his teeth. Through 1949, Byron drove strictly stock-class cars to victory at the Beach Road Course in Daytona on July 10, taking the lead in the last six laps. He managed to finish high in the standings in the rest of the year's races to emerge the Strictly Stock Champion.

But it was the race in Charlotte, North Carolina, on June 19, 1949, that started it all, and NASCAR's crowd-pleasing Strictly Stock series was launched. Dirt-track racers found themselves behind the wheel of modern vehicles with brand identifications: Ford, Chevrolet, Hudson, Oldsmobile, Buick, most of the Detroit manufacturers. Drivers such as Junior Johnson, Tim and Fonty Flock, Lee Petty, Ralph Earnhardt, Gober Sosbee, and Red Byron. Nibbling at the edges were a few pioneer women drivers such as Louise Smith behind the wheel of her Number 94 Nash Ambassador.

There would be a constant tinkering with the formula to develop a consistent winning race car under the stock rules. At Charlotte, there was a considerable variety of vehicles zipping and lumbering around that track. Nimble Chevrolets and Fords dodged in and out of the paths of big Oldsmobiles, Buicks, Hudson Hornets, Nash and Lincoln sedans. The bigger cars were thought to be more durable, able to take the pounding of a long race. Though Jim Roper ultimately won the race in a big Lincoln over a Ford that was disqualified because of a beefed-up suspension, Lee Petty had a more typical experience.

Petty was the patriarch of what became a racing dynasty with his sons, Richard and Maurice. He drove a bakery delivery truck for a paycheck and a huge Buick Roadmaster to the races. During the Charlotte race, his Buick was slammed into a crunching rollover. While the car's heft saved Lee from injury, it was totaled. Lee and his two sons had to hitch rides back to their home in Level Cross, North Carolina.

Helping sort the new rules and sanctioning racetracks in the 1950s was NASCAR's first commissioner, Erwin "Cannonball" Baker. Born in Dearborn County, Indiana, in 1882, he drove just about everything on wheels—and when he drove, he usually broke records. A natural show-man—he started out his many careers as a vaudeville performer—Baker loved speed. He set 143 driving records beginning in 1910 through the 1930s on motorcycles and in cars of all descriptions. His rush across the continent aboard a motorcycle in 1914 earned him his Cannonball nick-name from an eastern sports writer comparing him to train engineer Casey Jones's Cannonball Express. By the time Baker put aside his two-wheel hog, he'd logged 5,500,000 miles in transcontinental runs. Revving up a Stutz Bearcat auto, he set out in 1915 from Los Angeles and broke the coast-to-coast speed record, arriving in New York City in 11 days, 7 hours, and 15 minutes. In 1926, he loaded up and drove a two-ton truck from New York to San Francisco in five days and two years later beat the 20th Century Limited Express train from New York to Chicago. The famed cross-country Cannonball Run is named after his exploits.

As a racer, he also drove in the Indianapolis 500 and piloted a few stock cars before slowing down a bit in his 70s to take over the NASCAR job. In the 1950s under Baker's stewardship, the Strictly Stock class was renamed The Grand Nationals.

The advent of the showroom cars with minimum modifications struck a chord with the racing public who turned out to cheer their favorite driver and the brand of car he drove. Dirt tracks, however, were unkind to Strictly Stock or Grand National cars with soft suspensions, slow steering, and a lot of extra metal. Their big engines had no advantage on the shorter dirt tracks where the likes of Ralph Earnhardt made a living every week. As Bill France Sr. struggled to gather together the loose society of dirt-track racers under the NASCAR franchise, a fellow named Harold Brasington in Darlington, South Carolina, had an idea.

Inspired by a trip to the famed Indianapolis Speedway where open-wheel cars—the thoroughbreds of racing—had zoomed around a two-mile oval since 1908, this heavy equipment businessman decided to build his own paved high-speed track. Darlington was in the middle of tobacco country near no major roads. It had nothing to recommend it as a tourist location or anything but a sleepy southern town. None of the dirt-track racers had any experience tearing around a track paved with asphalt. While the idea suggested higher speeds would be possible, what about tire wear and soft jouncy suspensions and steering without the sliding drift of the rear wheels in clay corners? Everybody *knew* how to drive dirt: point your nose into the bottom of the turn and let the rear wheels push your back end around through the turn. The learning curve on asphalt promised to be steep.

Brasington persisted. He didn't own the land in tobacco country where he set up shop. Farmer Sherman Ramsey offered 70 acres, but he had a minnow pond he did not want drained. This pond forced the bulldozers and graders to create a pear-shaped 1.25-mile track where turns one and two were sharp to miss the pond, but turns three and four at the other end swept grandly around the infield. Hemmed in by poured concrete walls and large grandstands, Brasington's racetrack just needed a sanctioned race.

He approached the Central States Racing Association (CSRA) in Columbus, Ohio, to run the event, but they could not put together a field of entries for the September 4, 1950, Labor Day start. Brasington then turned to Bill France Sr., and NASCAR accepted the job under their Grand Nationals banner working with CSRA. Suddenly, they had more cars entering than they ever imagined. Finally after a severe triage, thinning the field to the most deserving, a three-abreast start offered up 75 cars.

The grandstands were packed to overflowing and roads for miles around were jammed with a bumper-to-bumper traffic nightmare to see this Southern 500 race. No one was sure the cars could even last 500 miles. All the big names were there: Lee Petty, the Flock boys Tom, Tim and Fonty, as well as Red Byron, Fireball Roberts, Cotton Owens, Jack Smith, Curtis Turner, Buck Baker, Marshall Teague and leading from the front three was Gober Sosebee. When the flag dropped on that herd of good old boys, the roar of cars and audience was volcanic.

Engines accelerated, dust boiled up off the asphalt, cloaking every car in a haze as paint swapping started early. One driver likened the start to all of New York's taxicabs run amok. Hudson Hornets rumbled past Nash Ambassadors, and Cadillacs dueled with Chevrolets while Packards and Desotos shouldered their way through the field. Due to the size of the field, front-runners were catching up to back markers in a couple of laps. Lap counting and keeping track of leaders was a headache. The dust and traffic was so dense that drivers had a hard time seeing when to turn. Most often, they picked out track landmarks or a heap of debris that had once been a race car and turned left when they reached it.

Out of the pile, a brand new Plymouth owned by Bill France Sr., prepared by Hubert Westmoreland—who only changed the spark plugs and replaced the tires—and driven by Johnny Mantz emerged at the head of the wreckage following him to the finish line. And, as would be the case in subsequent NASCAR races, many of the competing drivers and owners were all over that car in a long postrace inspection to make sure none of the minimal rules were jiggered.

Meanwhile, the last of the spectators staggered home from the racing marathon, and the drivers either rolled their battered racers onto trailers or hit starter buttons and drove home. The promoters sat down with big chicken-eating grins and counted the ticket-sales money out of a big bucket. Gone were the days when drivers took home a box of Hav-a-Tampa cigars, a case of Penzoil, or a $2.50 coupon to a local menswear store. Significant money had shown up and everybody squatting around that bucket was alight with the possibilities.

Sure, the long 250- and 500-mile races were big draws, but they were expensive to back and not many tracks were long enough to stand the wear and tear caused by that many laps. In 1950, Bill France Sr. dreamed up the NASCAR Short Track Division with separate point standings, trophies, and a fund separate from the Grand National Races. This series of races was held on tracks of less than a half mile in length. This was NASCAR's fourth division after the Modified, Roadster, and Strictly Stock (Grand National) Divisions. The Sportsman cars were not current models and were allowed some modifications—but not as many as the Modified Division cars.

Creating Sportsman cars was less expensive than the fully tricked-out Modified cars with extremely modified engines favoring the Ford Flat-head crammed into pre–World War coupes. Quick-change rear ends were commonplace as were high-rise manifolds and a gaggle of multibarrel car-buretors. The Sportsman racers were almost stock with stock carburetors, manifolds, and rear ends bolted on.

The original Daytona, Florida, track hosted the first Sportsman Division race in 1951 with more than 100 owners coming up with entry money. Later, in 1952 the Daytona track pitted Sportsman cars against the more powerful Modified racers. Running head-to-head, the Modified cars came out on top, but the Sportsmen finished as high as 12th across the line. Three to four Sportsman races were held each week totaling about 60 races a year.

One driver who embraced the Sportsman Division cars on their short tracks was Ralph Earnhardt driving his own racer and cars owned by others. These NASCAR races migrated across the Mississippi River to Ohio and Michigan in 1951 and 1952. Earnhardt competed as often as he could and won the 1956 Sportsman title. In 1958, he was laid up with a broken leg but returned eventually to the family business.

The creation of NASCAR was a boon to Ralph Earnhardt's racing career. The sanctioning body allowed him to move from Modified to both Sportsman and Grand National racing with those larger purses. Even with his mastering of the short tracks on both dirt and asphalt, he still managed to drive in 50 Grand National competitions, getting rides from high-profile car builders such as Lee Petty and Cotton Owens. Besides his 1956 Sportsman championship, he finished in the top-10 Sportsman point standings for six years and rolled into the 1960s in 17th place in the NASCAR Grand National point standings in 1961. Ralph Earnhardt brought home the winning purse over 100 times during his 23-year career with NASCAR.

It is difficult to imagine the stress and physical stamina required to climb behind the wheel—often five days a week—knowing he had to bring back a car that he could race the next day or the next and still race aggressively and intelligently to put food on the table and keep a roof over his family's head. At home, the little boy who kept track of Ralph's wins and losses by the condition of the car that rolled into the backyard after racing learned about the family business though the 1950s and '60s. During these formative years, Dale Jr. had a chance to watch his dad at the local races, to sit in the bed of the pickup truck, and absorb like a sponge, the talk, the sights, and the sounds of racing.

# Chapter 5

# THE LEARNING CURVE

For all the success that rewarded NASCAR innovators, there was still a steep learning curve to discover the magic formula of consistency without boredom and experimentation to produce new racing concepts. The Grand National and Sportsman races had found great support. This was due in almost equal proportions to the explosive temperaments and wild lifestyles of the mostly southern drivers and to the cars themselves, the recognizable brands of cars that could be found parked on any main street on either side of the Mississippi River.

Bill France headed up north in 1951 with his NASCAR traveling circus and brought a menagerie of drivers and taped-up stockish Grand National cars to Detroit, the Motor City where just about everything behind the start line began life as raw steel, glass, and rubber. Most were hauled around by push-rod iron V-8 engines, and they growled around the Michigan State Fairgrounds track behind the Packard pace car like an unruly, ill-mannered mob of prodigal children. The hot August 12th day warmed up their paintwork as the flag dropped and the 250th anniversary of the City of Detroit was celebrated with 250 miles of NASCAR madness. After covering 250 miles, Tommy Thompson from Kentucky lurched home the winner, concluding four hours of heavy attrition and pocketing $5,000 and a brand new Packard.

The bigger outcome of that race was the parade of Detroit executives who saw firsthand the crowd appreciation and the potential for an entirely new marketing direction. On another front, NASCAR began to spread to tracks that had never seen much stock car racing short of demolition derbies, those races where the object was to be the last car still running.

The stock car drivers began to emerge as the bad-boy rock stars of sport, and the growing media attention began to create legends.

While Ralph Earnhardt earned the nicknames Ironheart for his stamina and dogged pursuit of prize purses and also Mr. Consistency for developing a patient race plan that produced victories, there were the flashier drivers who lived large and drove the same way. There were a lot of stars who worked their way up through the pack in the 1950s and '60s, but a few stand out. Earnhardt was always ready to swap paint and drive hard if someone was between him and that checkered flag going into the last tow laps, but there were also drivers who only knew how to drive flat out until they won or turned their car into smoldering junk. Others had flashy styles and driving tricks that propelled them to fame. Some made their car brands famous and in demand just because they drove them so well.

Junior Johnson drove like the devil was in his rearview mirror. He was a former whiskey tripper who eventually served some time for his sins, but NASCAR probably saved his life when it gave him a track to run on and some horsepower to plow into the road.

He drove for owners as well as manufacturers, and drove his own cars when he could afford them, letting other young wannabes get behind the wheel. During his racing days, drivers said the worse thing they could see in their rearview mirrors was Junior's serious look as he swung in behind them bent on getting past—either around, over, or through—their cars.

Tom Wolfe's short story "The Last American Hero" gives the New Journalism–spin to Junior's tale and to the popularity of American stock car racing. Wolfe paints the racer's portrait upon arrival at a racetrack ready for business:

> Then, finally, here comes Junior Johnson. How he does come on. He comes tooling across the infield in a big white dreamboat, a brand new white Pontiac Catalina four-door, hard-top sedan. He pulls up and as he gets out he seems to get more and more huge. First his crew-cut head and then big jaw and them a bigger neck and then a huge torso, like a wrestler's all done up rather modish and California modern, with a red-and-white-candy-striped sport shirt, white ducks and loafers.
>
> "How you doin'?" says Junior Johnson, shaking hands, and then he says, "Hot enough for ye'uns?"[1]

Whenever Junior Johnson switched cars, the buzz around the tracks was electric. He switched from a Dodge to a Ford and then ran a Chevrolet, beating all comers, or wrecking in a Chevy without manufacturer sponsorship. People would go to see a race Junior was driving just to bet not on where he would finish, but if he would finish. He ran that lonesome Chevy against Fords, Plymouths, Dodges, and Mercurys, built by companies that had millions of dollars invested in drivers, cars, tires, mechanics, support services, whatever it took. But it took more than all that to beat Junior Johnson and his orphan Chevrolet Number Three. He won at Atlanta; Darlington; Charlotte; Bristol, Tennessee; and Martinsville, Virginia. He won himself out of the need to win because he invested his purses in that chicken ranch with a population of 42,000 fryers pecking corn instead of delivering moonshine by the jarful to thirsty clients in Wilkes County. He also owned a road-grading business. Who knows more about making roads better than somebody who spent time roaring on stiff springs through the clay cuts at night with a full load of moonshine whiskey, peering ahead into the fog for police roadblocks?

Other drivers turned it on when the green flag fell, created their legend between the concrete walls and the infield pits, and then turned it off when the checkered flag dropped. They were the technical wizards who survived on touch and feel and that ability to see the air between cars.

Chris Turner typified the "touch" drivers who dominated both dirt and asphalt tracks, getting the most out of his car and tires. His NASCAR records are numerous. He won two Grand National races from the pole position (fastest car in time trials) in the same car by leading every lap. He won a race in Ashville, North Carolina, because he was in the only car still running on the track near the end. His record includes 25 wins in the same car in 1956 in the convertible division, 22 of them with the top down and—one of them in the Southern 500—three with a top welded on.

Starting out in dirt, Turner developed the power slide or drift through a corner that set the car up perfectly aimed down the straightaway coming out of the turn. He rarely had to lift his foot off the gas and pounded his cars unmercifully in the mold of Junior Johnson, but he also had finesse. On the track his nickname was Pops. This had nothing to do with age, but referred to the way he popped (rammed the back bumpers) other drivers on the track. Sadly, he was also a party animal and a drinker to excess, two strikes that did not help his career. He was a personal friend of Bill France Sr., but that didn't help him when he tried to organize a union for drivers in 1961. He was banned from racing for life by France but was restored to driving status in 1965.[2]

With the variety of automobiles racing in the Grand Nationals, drivers became identified with certain makes, so much so that a shiver of apprehension shot through Junior Johnson's fans when in 1963 he shifted his loyalties from Dodge to Ford and then to Chevrolet—even when Chevrolet had dropped out of the racing business. Tim Flock drove a rare four-door Black Phantom Oldsmobile in 1951 instead of the two-door coupes favored by most drivers. The Hudson Hornet was the car of choice for Herb Thomas, who won 48 races and the Grand National Championship in both 1951—collecting $2,264.50 of the $40,000 total purse awards for that year—and 1953.

Experimentation didn't stop with the drivers. Bill France Sr. kept the Modified and Sportsman Divisions going to provide races for the drivers such as Ralph Earnhardt and owners who built their cars and didn't have the deep pockets to compete in the Grand Nationals with current models off the assembly line in Detroit. He created a Convertible Division in 1956, partnering with the Midwestern sanctioning group Society of Autosports and Fellowship Education (SAFE). NASCAR convertible racing lasted until 1959 when it officially shut down. The concept flopped because the cars were not as fast as the enclosed cockpit autos, or as safe in a crash—even with the added roll bars. They were heavy because of the additional built-in bracing to compensate for the lack of a hard top, and they were also a rich man's car. The division's one saving grace was visibility. There were no driver blind spots caused by pillars or posts used to support a hard top, and fans could see into the car and watch the drivers maneuver the wheel, work the gears, shake fists, and wave howdy. Convertibles were closer to Indianapolis roadsters before the European rear-engine cars shoved the driver up front to become nothing more than a helmeted bubble where the hood ornament used to be. In-car TV cameras gave all types of racing a new fan base at home. Convertibles continued to run on the Darlington Speedway through the early 1960s, but in novelty races.

During the 1957 Convertible Division races, Ralph Earnhardt strapped on a brand new Oldsmobile 88. Part of his crew was mechanic Richard Petty, Lee Petty's son and the next generation of that racing dynasty that rivaled the Earnhardts.

Another concept that came and went quickly was the NASCAR Speedway Division. To try and draw fans from Indianapolis open-wheel racing, France created this division in 1952. Indy-type roadster shells were shorn of their Offenhauser high-performance engines and refitted with standard Detroit mills—keeping car manufacturers interested. The first race was held at Darlington Raceway and the ubiquitous Buck Baker won tooling his roadster around the track for 200 miles hauled by a Cadillac engine. Baker was a fixture in NASCAR during his long career, running in 640 races and winning 46 times. He was Grand Nationals Champion in 1956 and 1957. The next Speedway race at Martinsville featured only 17 cars and Tex Keene came from last place to win behind a stock Mercury power plant.

The Langhorne Speedway in Pennsylvania hosted a 100-mile open-wheel event on their virtually circular tack called The Big Left Turn in June 1952. It was won by Tom Cherry. After a total of seven races, Buck Baker was declared the champion and the division was packed up and put away for good.[3] Open-wheel racing was considered too exotic and Eastern for the crowds down South. That year was tough on automakers in general facing a nationwide steel strike and a steamy hot summer. This was before auto air conditioning.

Langhorne Speedway developed a reputation for sampling NASCAR's experiments. Wanting to be all-inclusive and acknowledging the postwar importation of foreign-made autos into the United States, NASCAR created International races. These contests involved a mixture of domestic and foreign entries typified by Langhorne's International 200 held in June 1953. A Jaguar driven by Lloyd Shaw sat on the pole when the flag dropped, but it eventually dropped back to 23rd. Another Jaguar finished 6th, driven by Dick Allwine, followed by two Porches in 8th and 9th place with a real long-shot 1952 Volkswagen driven by Dick Hagey racing from 32nd to 19th place.[4]

On January 20, 1952, at the Palm Beach Speedway in Florida, the season opening 100-mile race won by Tim Flock was almost fatally marred. Bernard Alvarez flipped his Oldsmobile onto its roof, crushing it flat. He escaped injury, but the accident moved NASCAR to require all cars to have steel rollover bars installed to prevent such roof cave-ins. The following month, Tim Flock drove his 1939 Ford to victory at Daytona but was disqualified in the mandatory postrace technical inspection for having improper roll bars supporting his roof.

In that same race, the first use of two-way radio-to-pits communications was logged. Al Stevens, who operated a radio dispatch service in Maryland, kept in contact with his pit boss, Cotton Bennett, throughout the race, managing to bring his car in 6th place in the Sportsman Class and 23rd overall.

Trying to establish consistency among the eccentric and free-spirited drivers to fit into a more professional NASCAR mold was like trying to herd cats. The very nature of a race driver is rooted in individuality. After winning the Southern 500 at Darlington from halfway back in the pack on September 1, 1952, Fonty Flock, brother of Tim and Tom, stopped on the track's front stretch in front of the main grandstand and clambered up onto the roof. There, clad in his racing clothes—Bermuda shorts and a short-sleeve shirt—he led the audience in singing *Dixie*, the Southern National Anthem.

Carl Kiekhaefer, a millionaire businessman selling Mercury Outboard Motors, assembled one of the earliest team racing concepts in the 1950s. He had his identical cars painted in the same color scheme as were the transporter trucks for each car, and he provided matching uniforms to crew and drivers alike. He brought buckets of money into the sport and by 1955 sponsored seven cars. He insisted on curfews and the unheard-of banishment of drivers' wives to opposite ends of the motel on the day before the race. He developed the team racing concept that would eventually spread through all of NASCAR. This was the exact opposite of the lone-wolf driver/owners such as Dale Earnhardt and Junior Johnson. But the old era was slow to die. Junior Johnson won five races in that same year.

Tom Flock, dazzled by Kiekhaefer's Chrysler 300, drove for the millionaire, winning 18 races in 1955, but fled in 1956. He was replaced by Buck Baker and Herb Thomas. The implied precision and squeaky clean habits of the Kiekhaefer team were evident as its drivers won 21 of the first 25 races in 1956. But all was not well in the rank and file. Herb Thomas quit and revolving door–driver changes made the team concept questionable. Finally, the money buckets developed holes and the return on Kiekhaefer's investment in racing failed to sufficiently improve his bottom line. After all the sound and fury of his invasion into American stock car racing, the outboard motor king left the sport after the 1956 season.[5]

But his ideas of pouring parts, money, and tech support into the sport had caught on. The late 1950s saw an increase in Detroit's interest in making its brands winners in front of those postwar, car-hungry fans. On the horizon, the Eisenhower administration in Washington mandated a new interstate highway system as a bolster to American security giving the military speedier access to move men and material across the continent as needed. These six-lane superhighways also anticipated faster cars with bigger engines to move citizens for vacations and other family travels. Fuel was cheap, and new fluid drives and automatic transmissions were making cars easier to use. Suburbs for returning Korean War vets were opening up outside cities, and Americans were spending more time on the road, more time in their cars. Cars were becoming integral with America's culture, and the crowds attending races were growing. Supporting NASCAR was just good business.

During the 1950s, however, one speed bump almost scuttled racing altogether. As manufacturers bought into stock car racing, horsepower became a big selling point for every make. Detroit began offering speed packages for its showroom models and since the packages came from the car makers, the cars using them could be considered stock. Fuel injection and superchargers showed up and speeds climbed. Hyperbole among the advertising agencies also began to soar, and NASCAR passed rules against false advertising and using race results in ads. Any manufacturer violating these rules lost points in the championship race. Both Ford and Chevrolet found themselves penalized.

Corporate involvement in NASCAR racing demanded winners justify the staggering amount of money Detroit was plowing into research and development for their very public racetrack competitions. The car makers took what they learned on the track and adapted technology to their showroom models. NASCAR sought to keep the flow of knowledge feeding back into their race cars. In the 1950s drivers were consulted by Detroit engineers and executives to learn what was required to win on the track. Ford executives asked driver Buddy Shuman to visit their offices and discuss how to win races. His suggestions were mostly put aside because he wanted technology that had not been tested on the track—not Ford's usual practice and in direct opposition to General Motors' winning formula. Even so, in 1955 Ford Motors executive Bill Benton had two custom Fords built for the Southern 500 at Darlington and hired Curtis Turner and Joe Weatherby to pilot the hybrids. Neither finished the race because of breakdowns and, to make things worse, a Chevrolet driven by Herb Thomas won the race for his third Southern 500 victory.

As the manufacturers labored to find the magic formula, drivers struggled to keep up with the pace and grueling demands of racing week after week. During World War II and in Korea, amphetamines, marketed under the label Benzedrine, had been used to keep soldiers fighting and to battle fatigue. During the 1950s, when the drug became available legally to the public, its use became widespread among athletes, truck drivers, and anyone under heavy stress to accelerate their capabilities. Many race car drivers—and not just those piloting stock cars—popped dextroamphetamine (dexadrine or just dex) and methamphetamine (meth, uppers, speed) before races. Some drivers, already steadied by whiskey, then jump-started their systems with pills and climbed into cars capable of 150-mile-per-hour speeds.

The result was shortened careers, either by bone-crushing accidents or heart attacks and fainting from soaring blood pressure. Fans cheered their favorite drivers, like Curtis Turner, who even grabbed snorts of whiskey *during* the race. Bill France Sr., who needed to control all of NASCAR, figured the only way to clean up the situation was to bring in more money through corporate sponsorship. For a driver to be suspended for breaking any rules and missing high-paying purses, or being fired from teams that paid well would be a hard punishment, especially for drivers trying to make a living behind the wheel.

And then at the Virginia 500 on the Martinsville Speedway on May 19, 1957, a car roared out of control on lap 441 of the 500-lap race, hurtled across a wall, and came down amid spectators who had infiltrated the no-spectators-permitted area. Several people went to the hospital. The track was one of the first paved superspeedways emphasizing high-speed straights, hard-braking turns, and rapid acceleration.[6] The media ganged up and demanded a ban on all racing. Following the media lead, the Automobile Manufacturers Association demanded that all manufacturers withdraw their support for the sport that emphasized speed and horsepower. Almost overnight Detroit-sponsored racing teams melted away and money evaporated.

In a very short time, the sport was tossed back on the pre–Grand National days when the salty dirt-track drivers running their skeletonized Modified and tape-covered Sportsman cars ruled stock car racing. Bill France offered up appearance money—about $300—to keep the big stars running in his races. The drivers called it travel money. The problem was the drivers who were the biggest names were getting too old for competition and chose to own cars, but not race them. Many of these older racers found themselves without any cash support and could barely afford to pay crews on race days or mechanics to keep their cars in competition trim. Running current model cars week after week and remaining competitive was almost impossible.

For John Holman, a former Ford executive who replaced Bud Shuman running Ford's East Coast racing program and driver Ralph Moody, the Detroit split from NASCAR became a huge opportunity. Ford suddenly was stuck with a huge inventory of cars and racing equipment for their stable of 8 or 10 cars. Holman-Moody set up shop in Charlotte, North Carolina, and began selling parts and building race cars for about $5,000 apiece. Their race teams went on to win a lot of races and gave rides to the best drivers in the business. They literally held NASCAR together during the manufacturers' revolt that ran out of gas by the end of the 1950s when Chevrolet began under-the-table support, and in 1962, Ford came back big time sponsoring four teams.[7]

While this sudden vacuum developed in Grand National Division racing, the withdrawal of manufacturers had little effect on Ralph Earnhardt except where larger purses were concerned. He continued to be the man to beat on any short dirt or paved track on which he chose to compete. He had moved on to Grand Nationals. He competed in 16 NASCAR races,

11 of which ran Grand National cars, including current model Fords and Oldsmobiles. These cars were owned by Pete DePaolo, Petty Enterprises, Petty Engineering, and the Woods Brothers. From the Grand National races, Ralph earned about $1,835 for the decade. In modern dollars, this is the equivalent of $13, 562.49. Besides the Grand National races, Ralph continued to race his 1937 and 1939 Modified cars, built cars for other drivers, and tested tires. He continued to race day after day, week after week, on dozens of "crappy little tracks,"[8] and it aged him.

The last year of the 1950s proved to be a watershed for the racing sport. Through the 1950s Bill France Sr. had promised the creation of a super-speedway, and it was going to happen in Daytona where NASCAR got its start in the late 1940s and where a beach-racing culture had flour-ished. The Daytona Beach Road course had become a sport unto itself as southern boys powered through its first sweeping turn just to keep going sideways straight into the ocean.

Daytona had regained its place as a racing institution after being abandoned by the land- speed record seekers for the more remote, more forgiving Bonneville Salt Flats in Utah. The course had at least three con-figurations, but the most famous had been conceived back in 1936, when Highway A1A paralleling the ocean was graded with a left turn leading to the hard-packed sandy shore, then a race past the waves and another left to reconnect with the highway.

Fans parked their cars between the highway and the beach stretch called the infield. Stock cars could rumble 12 abreast down the shore stretch, shoving and clambering to funnel down to two or three abreast for the turn. The tide played a factor too. The race had to be started when the tide was out to create the shore stretch, and the race had to end before the tide came back in. On windy days, a race could be called because of large ocean waves. Dirt-track rules applied through the turns. Experienced drivers set up for the turn a half mile before they arrived. At two tenths of a mile before entering the sandy grooves, the driver turned his car side-ways, swinging the car's stern toward the outside of the track. The result-ing drift carried the car through the sand until it pointed straight down the seashore.[9] Now take this careful choreography and do it at speed, in traffic, with a salt-spattered windshield and mushy steering from all the sand kicked into every crevice. Rookies had a very steep learning curve. The paved highway stretch didn't offer much of a breather. It only mea-sured 22-1/2 feet wide—hardly conducive to passing.

Everybody yearned to be a front-runner at Daytona; otherwise, they ate a lot of sand. Over a long race, the incessant sand literally sand-blasted the paint off the front of the car and pitted the windshield. Some drivers reinstalled what had disappeared from most NASCR racers over the years, a good windshield wiper. In place of the wiper, other drivers carried small mops in the car. When the pace of action allowed, they reached out and swept off the sand for a clear view of the track ahead. Of course, the sand-grooved turns turned into a bog over the course of the race, so each turn became a new adventure. If the car was overheating, the driver could swing a bit wide on the turn-exit and splash through the surf for a few yards to cool the engine. Of course, the salt water caused its own problems.

The spectators were another hazard. They were everywhere: on the beach shore, in the infield, crowding around the turns, and even freeloading offshore by bobbing in their boats without paying admission. The 4.1-mile length and acreage around it allowed for many trespassers, so Bill France planted signs at regular intervals among the dunes that read "Beware of Rattlesnakes."[10]

Over time, Florida real estate had encroached deeply into the area around the Daytona Beach racetrack, and Bill France was determined to follow up on his brag back in 1954 to create a superspeedway. If France had no other skills, his ability to squeeze money and favors from high rollers was legendary. His vision was for a 2.5-mile oval track at least as big as the Indianapolis Motor Speedway, all paved and wider than any track then in existence. The parcel of land selected was next to the Daytona Beach airport and was sodden with swamps. With a price tag topping $2 million, France sold stock shares in his International Speedway Corporation, borrowed heavily, and put up his house for loan collateral. But when the track was ready for inspection by the drivers, they were in awe of its size, its high-speed banked turns, and the potential for very fast racing.

The first race on the Daytona International Speedway lasted three days. It was a 500-mile race that France cooked up against most advice. He mixed convertibles with sedans as a gimmick for the spectators, but the blend did nothing for the quality of the race. During tests, running hard on the new track, drivers had noticed that they managed to go an average of three miles per hour faster when running with traffic than they did on solo qualifying heats. This increase in speed was attributed to the effect called drafting. The aerodynamics of the cars caused the wind to slide over the surface and rush off the trunk, creating a temporary vacuum immediately behind the car. This vacuum sucked the following car into its airstream, reducing the drag on the rear of the lead car and drawing along the trailing car—increasing the speed of both cars. It took some nerve to stick the nose of the car into the draft, but the advantage of speed over the field and being in position to pass should the lead car suffer a lapse of any kind was worth the maneuver. At the higher speeds permitted by the superspeedways, drafting became the winning strategy.

Sadly, in that opening race, February 22, 1959, convertibles qualified separately from the sedans and were then combined for the big show. Only when combined, as the cars roared around the paved surface, was it evident that the draft didn't work for the rag tops, which had no enclosed capsule shape like the sedans and, therefore, no aerodynamic airflow. The convertibles found themselves being lapped by faster sedans about every 10 laps as they careened their lonely way around the speedway.

Richard Petty in an Oldsmobile nosed out Johnny Beauchamp's Thunderbird at the finish line. However, Beauchamp got the win, the trophy, the trip to victory lane, and the kiss from the pretty girl, and Petty retired to his hotel. Confusion and consternation reigned, and it took three days of studying photographs to verify that it was indeed Petty's win. Bill France called him personally to announce the reversal of fortunes.

Though racing remained popular in the time of Detroit's abandoning the field, sponsorship money was thin on the ground. While Holman-Moody kept racing teams competing, drivers had to find new revenue generators. Junior Johnson had invested his winnings in his Holly Farms chicken ranch. Other drivers worked out consulting and testing deals with the manufacturers. Pontiac had snared Fireball Roberts while Lee Petty had inked agreements with Oldsmobile and Plymouth. Another team entered the lists in 1960 headed by Wood, a car driver/owner. He and his younger brother Leonard and siblings Delano, Ray Lee, and Clay had created Woods Brothers Racing in 1955. Their winning ways came from hiring good drivers and also pioneering precisely drilled and crisply executed pit stops. They set the pattern for real team racing, shaving seconds off time spent in the pits. On April 24, 1959, at the Southern States Fairgrounds, the brothers sent out a 1958 Ford Convertible. At the wheel was hard charger Ralph Earnhardt.

One of the fixtures on the Woods Brothers team was Marvin Panch. He drove 81 races for the brothers and was considered a very competent driver if not a superstar. In 1963, having qualified for the Daytona 500, Panch received an offer he couldn't refuse. Like most drivers, always short of cash, he signed on for a ride in a Maserati 151—a high-performance sports car that normally raced at Sebring, LeMans, and other road tracks. The owners had installed a Grand Nationals 7-litre Ford push-rod V-8 in place of the smaller exotic 5.6-litre engine and needed a driver for the American Challenge Cup, the usual opening act for the 500-mile race. Panch knew that Bill France offered a $10,000 prize for the first driver to reach a speed over 180 miles per hour. After taking the car out for a test spin, Panch didn't like its handling. The Woods Brothers chief mechanic, Leonard Wood, conferred with Panch and tweaked the Maserati for the attempted record.

Sliding into the low-slung road racer, Panch set off, running up through the gears, hauling coal down the straights, and powering through the steeply banked turns one and two. Howling into turn three, the road racer hurtled into the air. Airborne, it turned over and crashed down onto its roof. Both doors opened from the top, and they were crushed shut by the impact. Scouring the pavement, shearing sparks, tearing the air with the rasp of tortured metal, the Maserati slid to a stop and burst into flame. Firemen arrived, but the flames were out of control. Trapped inside the scorching cockpit, Panch drummed on the unyielding door with his shoulders, feet, fists, anything to keep from roasting alive. At that moment, Dewayne 'Tiny" Lund arrived with four other drivers. Lund threw his 6-foot 6-inch, 300-pound frame at the car and, as its paint bubbled and Panch continued to thrash at his prison, Tiny lifted the car far enough to allow access to one of the doors. With a second effort, he reached in through the side window and heaved Panch out of the inferno, and they both fell back just as the gas tank exploded, temporarily blinding Steve Petrasek, one of the other rescuers. Tiny Lund received the Carnegie Medal of Honor for saving Marvin Panch's life.

But the story continued. Panch's injuries, though not life-threatening, forced him to give up his ride for the Woods Brothers in the 500-mile race. Lund was a journeyman driver and had neither car nor sponsor, so the Woods Brothers offered him Panch's car with their gratitude. The predicted winner of the 1963 race was supposed to be Freddie Lorenzen, the latest hot star, driving a Holman-Moody Ford. Tiny Lund wheeled Panch's car out onto the track, won the Daytona 500, and locked himself into the legends of NASCAR.

The superspeedway had proved to be the shot in the arm needed to keep public attention and attendance focused on stock car racing while the car manufacturers had reduced their participation to back-alley deals, and third-party teams prospered. As the big paved tracks blossomed, short dirt tracks with limited cash saw their schedules reduced. Attendance at the small tracks dropped off as the racing stars sought out the bigger pay-checks for fewer races. Also, by this time, television had found its way into the rural South. Watching Ed Sullivan's *Toast of the Town* or Arthur Godfrey's *Talent Scouts* after the hogs were fed began replacing a ride to the local half-mile track.

Television—and the rest of the national media—had pretty much ignored stock car racing as being too regional except for novelty local shows featuring the ever-popular demolition derbies. Twelve and sixteen-inch screens bloomed in darkened living rooms from the Deep South to the Midwest with images of clapped-out junkers on their last legs lumbering around dirt tracks deliberately hammering into each other, sending pieces flying. The winner would be the last dented wreck that could complete a lap while shorn of fenders, steam-geysering from a punctured radiator, its trunk sprung and flapping obscenely. That's how many Americans saw stock car racing.

And then in 1960, CBS approached the Daytona 500 to produce a live telecast of the pole-position qualifying race and the compact-car race prior to the big 500-mile event. On January 31, 1960, a minimum TV crew, black-and-white cameras, and the on-camera host Bud Palmer arrived. NBC heard of the CBS effort and immediately hustled together a crew that arrived at Daytona to televise a 4-mile, 10-lap sprint called the Autolite Challenge Race. The electrical system supplier handpicked the drivers and turned them loose.

On February 13, after the TV crews packed up, 73 Sportsman Division cars took off on a 250-mile race, part of Daytona Speed Week. As the cars rushed down off the fourth turn, Dick Foley's car slew sideways, and he fought the wheel to straighten out. He managed to correct the slide, but behind him 37 other cars were not so lucky. In a whirling melee of bodies, chassis, tires, big and little bits of NASCAR Sportsman racers, the home straight turned into a huge scrap yard. A dozen cars sailed through the air, smashing, crashing, and caroming off other cars until 24 of the 37 involved vehicles were totaled. Eight drivers were shipped to the hospital, none with serious injuries. The following Daytona 500 was also a punishing event, running 30 laps under the yellow caution flag. By the time Speed Week ended, the Grand National drivers and teams were in such bad shape, NASCAR canceled the next two scheduled races until the trash dragged off the track could be reassembled into race cars.

On the day before "the big one" entered into NASCAR jargon, one driver possibly had his life saved by NASCAR rules. Herman Beam had the dubious honor of being the first driver to be black flagged—ordered off the race course—by NASCAR officials during the pair of 100-mile qualifying heats. His rule infraction caused him to miss the next day's race. He had forgotten to put on his helmet.

The superspeedways continued to be big attendance draws during 1960, and 9 of the 44 races held that year were held on the new fast tracks. Another result of the new facilities and television's interest in stock car racing was Detroit's revival of overt participation in the sport. Though they had been unofficially giving aid to the teams who used their cars, the sport's growing popularity west of the Mississippi, on the West Coast, and north into the Midwest sparked reconsideration. Hard-core adherence to the Automobile Manufacturer's Association 1957 ban on stock car–racing support—though given lip service by its members—was fading away by 1960. Fueled by the revenue realities offered by promotions, increasing sales opportunities, and technological advances, General Motors and Ford both hired spies to begin skulking about and peering over each other's back fence.

Ford Motors won 15 times and General Motors captured 20 victories during the year, including the Daytona 500, the World 600 at Charlotte, and the Grand National Championship. Even Chrysler's modest program partnering with Petty Engineering picked up nine wins. Big changes seemed to be on the way.

## NOTES

1. Tom Wolfe, "The Last American Hero is Junior Johnson. Yes!" *Esquire*, March 1965.

2. Mike Hembree, NASCAR: *The Definitive History of American Sport* (New York: Harper Entertainment, 2000), pp. 64–66.

3. William Burt, *The American Stock Car* (St. Paul: MN: MBI Publishing, 2001), p. 34.

4. Bleacher Report, "NASCAR History: The Good Old Days, Pennsylvania Style," http://bleacherreport.com/articles/27976-nascar-history-the-good-old-days-pennsylvania-style; How Stuff Works, "How NASCAR Race Cars Work," http://www.entertainment.howstuffworks.com/nascar.htm.

5. Hembree, pp. 68–69.

6. One Bad Wheel, "Martinsville Speedway," http://www.onebadwheel.com/martinsville-speedway-nascar/track/.

7. Joe Menzer, *The Wildest Ride: A History of NASCAR* (New York: Simon & Schuster, 2001), pp. 134–138.

8. Auto Racing Daily, "Dale Jr. Talks About His Father, Career and Marriage," http://www.autoracingdaily.com/news/latest-racing-news/dale-jr-talks-about-his-father-career-and-marriage/.

9. Hembree, p. 72.

10. Ibid., pp. 73–74.

# Chapter 6

# WINDING DOWN
# AND WINDING UP

In 1961 the Charlotte Motor Speedway needed a considerable loan to remain financially stable so it went to the Teamsters Union, then led by Jimmy Hoffa, for about $850,000. In return for the loan, Hoffa suggested that the race drivers should have their rights ensured by joining the union. Curtis Turner accepted the job of persuading the drivers from NASCAR, the United States Auto Club, and the Midwest Association of Race Cars (later ARCA—the American Race Car Association) to join up. Sentiment had always been simmering below the surface over Bill France's dictatorial control of NASCAR, so the convinced drivers formed the Federation of Professional Athletes (FPA). The loan was approved and Turner issued a statement announcing the drivers' decision to join the Teamsters through the FPA.

Bill France Sr. detonated. In a statement to the press and at a meeting with drivers, he stated his position: "No known Teamster member will compete in a NASCAR race, and I'll use a pistol to enforce that rule. Before I have this union stuffed down my throat, I will plow up my two and a half mile race track and plant corn in the infield."[1]

Curtis Turner, Fireball Roberts, and Tim Flock were bounced out of NASCAR for life. Roberts came bounding back, claiming he had misunderstood the harm the union would create, denounced the FPA, scratched out his membership, and was re-enfolded into the good graces of NASCAR at once. To create damage control, France and the NASCAR Board in turn formed the Grand National Advisory Board assigning two NASCAR executives, Ed Otto and Pat Purcell; two car owners, Rex Lovette and Lee Petty; a pair of promoters, Clay Earles and Enoch Staley; and two drivers,

Ned Jarrett and Rex White. These representatives were ombudsmen to oversee any problems among NASCAR members and to deal with issues brought up by the aborted union push.

Largely unaffected by this NASCAR in-fighting was Ralph Earnhardt. Though he had expanded into Grand National (GN) racing, driving for the Pettys and the Wood Brothers well into 1964, he remained a steadfast independent. The hoopla and bigness of the GN races was not for him. He had great records at tracks such the raceway in Greenville-Pickens Fairgrounds and at Hickory Speedway, but the fuss and feathers of Grand National racing, the grueling 500-mile races, and the long trips away from Kannapolis were tiring.

By the middle of the 1960s, he had a growing teenager at home who appeared to have two problems. First, young Dale Earnhardt wanted to bail out of school and second, he wanted to be a race driver. Ralph began to pull in his horns and confine his races to local tracks such as the Concord and Metrolina Speedways. There, he was practically guaranteed 20–30 wins a year and track championships against up-and-coming local talents. Besides building cars and working on engines for other drivers who came to his Speed & Custom shop out behind the house, Ralph continued to test tires for Humpy Wheeler.

Wheeler, at age 25 with a college education behind him, was a promoter and racetrack operator at heart, but due to the hassles of those jobs, including lawsuits from angry drivers and car owners for one thing or another, he was spinning his wheels. His experience finally landed him his dream job, director of racing for Firestone Tire & Rubber Company. That job got him involved with every kind of motor sport from Formula One road racing to Indy open-wheel roadsters and the new rear-engine cars from Europe. He saw all the tracks, met the drivers, and lived the life. During the 1960s, stock car racing was still thought of as strictly a redneck[2] sport by the racing industry. But for the tire and rubber companies, the big powerful cars meant big business.

Winners on the racetrack sold new cars—and tires—out of the showroom. It was not uncommon for a Grand National car to go through 10 sets of tires in a long race as track conditions changed and the rubber was scrubbed off the chord by the high-speed turns, braking, and acceleration. Rubber compounds for tires became critical to winning races, depending on the surface they ran on, the weather, and the way the car suspension was set up for the particular track.

As mentioned earlier, Ralph Earnhardt was one of the earliest drivers to make use of what came to be called stagger in setting up the car's four wheels.

The tires themselves—especially in dirt-track racing—contribute to performance depending on how they match the extreme variations of the track surface from wet to dry and hot to cold. The grooves in the tire, besides adding grip against centrifugal force, carry away heat. The number of grooves and their depth are critical as are rubber compounds, varying from soft for wet tracks to hard for when the tracks dry out. The flexibility or rigidity of the wrapped chord that supports the rubber contributes to the tire's durability over a long race where the car's weight shifts rapidly from side to side. A tire tester required expert judgment.

It wasn't long before Humpy Wheeler asked Ralph to test tires for Firestone. They had a long time together to get to know each other, and Wheeler gave Earnhardt credit for quitting the steady but plodding work at the Cannon Mills factory for racing. As far as Humpy could tell, considering the inexact records of the smaller tracks, Ralph won more than 250 races. During Wheeler's time at Firestone, Ralph became his "chief, dirt track, southern, weekly test driver."[3] A load of tires would be delivered and later Humpy would call Ralph for his verdict. If the tires performed well, Earnhardt's laconic reply would be, "Not bad." If they almost put him into the wall, he'd drawl, "You might want to look into that a little bit more."[4]

In the late 1960s, the town of Kannapolis, North Carolina, was a boomtown of sorts. Fieldcrest Cannon Mills, the largest textile mill in the world, was spread out over acres of real estate and provided steady employment for thousands turning out sheets and towels and, like most blue-collar southern towns, its wages fueled a car culture. Virtually everybody's backyard had a car in it, many in states of repair or beautification. The blatting of unmuffled engines was so common nobody paid any attention. So the grinding, rumbling, clanking sounds coming from Ralph Earnhardt's garage out behind the white bungalow at 1412 Sedan Avenue were just part of the village fabric. Driving up and down Cadillac Street, Plymouth Street, Desoto Street, or Buick Street tells you just about everything you need to know about the car section of Greater Kannapolis.

Today, there's a nine-foot-tall statue of Dale Earnhardt in the Kannapolis Mall square at town center surrounded by an oval walkway and visited by picture-taking tourists. You walk on the names of local citizens and fans engraved in the individual bricks that make up the hushed shrine. Dale's mother, Ralph's widow, Martha, still lives in the two-story bungalow with a steep-sloping roof that she and her husband moved into 52 years earlier, and from her front porch, she can still see her Memorial Baptist Church. Her children carry the Earnhardt name that reaches back to 1724 in German genealogy.

The mills are gone and a college campus is being built on the site, but in this part of the country, this quiet village still carries some of the magic that began in those late 1960s when Ralph began giving young Dale, the third of his five children, a second look. Dale was growing into a big rangy kid with the built-in impatience of small-town boys to get something going, to find some action.

It is hard for a young man to follow in his father's footsteps. A natural rebellion exists between fathers and sons, a desire for the son to find his own identity. Fathers, if they are worth their salt, try to steer their boys away from the more harsh mistakes that intrude on growing up. Dale was six years old when Ralph won the 1956 NASCAR Sportsman Championship and accumulated all the honors that went with being the man to beat on short dirt tracks. Dale grew up with all the baggage that went with being Ralph Earnhardt's kid. In his case, the baggage amounted to expectations, the critical examinations to see if he packed the gear to succeed at any competitive enterprise.

One truth proved out. He was no scholar and, despite his father's pleas and threats, Dale quit school after the ninth grade. But mill towns didn't approve of layabouts. If you weren't in school, you got a job and as a teenager, he went to work as a linthead at the mill. The large textile factory rolled its machines six days a week, 24 hours a day, and when the men exited the vast complex with their empty lunch boxes, they went home to work on their cars. There were the usual baseball games or the movies. Dale liked to race his bicycle and he won a little eight-inch plastic trophy at age 13—his first—piloting a slot car racer at Frank Dayvault's slot car race track, D&D Model Raceway, on Main Street. Frank and his brother, Wayne, ran Dayvault's Tune Up and Brake Service. They were known for their mechanical skills until they moved to Myrtle Beach on the Carolina coast.

Slot car racing may sound like it's a far cry from the howling action of a superspeedway on a Sunday afternoon, but the competition is often fierce as cars only a few inches long sail over curves and straights, fastened by a pin in a slot to the road surface. The cars are often modified within certain weight and dimensional restrictions and throttle handling requires considerable skill at the high speeds.

In downtown Kannapolis, Frank Dayvault opened a race shop featuring two tracks: a figure eight and a road course. The tracks had eight lanes controlled by the drivers standing outside the track, remote-controlling the speed of the cars with a small hand throttle. Too much speed could spin out a car on the turns so a deft touch was needed. Dale had that kind of touch, figuring the speed into and out of the turns to get maximum performance on the straights.

With their interest in full-size race cars, Frank and Gregg Dayvault treated the slot car competitions with the same professional efficiency. When a slot car manufacturer brought out a small-scale dynamometer to test the cars' speeds, the Dayvaults had to have one. Dale often ran a model 1955 Chevy while Gregg raced a 1966 Ford Fairlane. The races became a regular Saturday event in town. To this day, Gregg Dayvault remembers the excitement of watching the cars zoom around the track, the smell of ozone from the electric motors, and the oil of wintergreen spread bright red on the rear wheels for better traction.

The Dayvaults also applied their car-building skills for a local legend, the slow-to-talk and hard-as-nails auto-shop owner Berl Eddleman. He was known throughout the hill country as a man who could squeeze the last amount of speed out of a new sedan or a salvaged crock. His gift for amping up horsepower was particularly appreciated by the whiskey trippers and bootleggers who managed fleets of fast cars. One of his assistants, working part time to feed and clothe a growing family, was Ralph Earnhardt. Flat-head 1940 Ford engines were the prime movers for the bootleggers, those and big Cadillac V-8 power plants shoehorned into the lightweight Ford coupes. Eddleman's customers were a varied lot from young race-driver wannabes souping up their street rods to the more sober serious whiskey trippers, who brought in their cars without license plates and preferred not to hang around while their cars were worked on. One good reason for anonymity was the assortment of police, who brought in their squad cars in order to jack up the horsepower.

"You didn't really talk to these people a lot, so you didn't know a lot about them," Dayvault said. "There were certain groups who told you too much, but not many. "Junior Johnson and his brothers . . . they didn't say much."

"Bootleggin', that was big business back then," said Johnson. "My neck of the woods and over in Virginia, that's where the roots of the sport are, and where it really took a hold years ago." Johnson and his brothers, Fred and L.P., would leave their customized Ford to Eddleman, and return to find a fire-breathing, shine-running beast with revived horses spilling out from under the hood. "We'd have to do that about every three or four months," Johnson says through a chuckle, perhaps remembering the harsh punishment those cars endured. "Never had any trouble with 'em; they'd just wear out. The engines were great. They knew what they were doing at Eddleman's. And at the particular time, I was just interested in going fast and hauling whiskey."[5]

Not far from Ralph Earnhardt's house on Sedan Street, Route 29 snakes around Kannapolis. According to Norris Dearman, historian at the

Charles Cannon Memorial Library, the auto-shop owners had staked out a measured mile and their handiwork could be heard blasting down the street, gas pedal pressed flat. According to Dayvault, the run was "kind of a 'flying mile'—we'd get a head start and hit the line running. The flathead Fords were good for about 34 seconds, which was like 108–110 miles per hour. A regular street Ford then would go about 85."[6]

Some cars were more risky than others. According to Dayvault, there was one car he tried on their flying mile that had the capability of reaching 120 miles per hour, finishing the run in 30 seconds. But it was a scary machine with touchy handling. Ralph volunteered to slide in behind the wheel and took off down Route 29 in a blast of exhaust. When he returned, he said the car "wanted to move around him," but he was the one driver who could handle it.

Robert Yates, a NASCAR veteran and acknowledged engine and horsepower expert for more than 30 years besides owning his own racing team, grew up around the Earnhardts. "Those people raced every weekend, right up until high school football started. Then they'd race on just Saturday nights until it got too cold." Yates was part of the after-school engine-building culture and turned those skills into a career. He and some friends were always tinkering with ways to extract speed from iron and steel on the short tracks like Concord and Metrolina. Their methods didn't always follow the rule book. When accused of continual cheating, most car owners protested vigorously.

As one team member remembers, "That's the biggest damn lie in the world. We got caught our first night against those guys; our engine was too far back. We made a special trip past their inspectors to ask them where we could locate the engine, and we did it."

With groceries riding on the outcome, there was no way anybody could convince Ralph Earnhardt if there was trickery going on. If he couldn't beat someone on the track, he found a way to get some satisfaction behind the scenes.

"It cost $100 to protest a race," remembers Dave Gray, a Robert Yates team member. "There'd be about 30 cars there—Ralph Earnhardt would go down and say, 'Boys, the 92 car is pretty fast tonight. You wanna go in $10 with me and protest 'em?' He'd get $10 from 13 or 14 people, put 40 in his pocket and put a hundred out there, and he'd make Robert pull the cylinder head every Friday night."[7]

It was hard to stay angry with Ralph Earnhardt and there was a constant one-upmanship among the drivers to take bread off the other guy's table. One of the teams ran a car with a spoiler wing on the rear deck. Earnhardt felt the spoiler was a useless doodad and went to war against it. During the race, he ran his car up tight behind the offensive car's stern and gave just enough bump to dislodge the wing from its brackets. Objecting to this treatment, the spoiler car's owner threatened retaliation. Earnhardt just grinned. "You don't need that damned spoiler," he said.

Not to be bullied, the team drove back to the garage that night and got out the bender used to shape the hollow steel tubes that make up the car's roll cage, which protects the driver. With the bender, they fashioned a huge, bulbous bumper on the front of their car and painted it bright orange. Its intended use was beyond question. The following Saturday night, Earnhardt stared at the battering ram bumper as the car offloaded from its trailer. He had met his match and gave the team that same goofy grin and a thumbs up.[8]

"He never messed with us again," laughed the car's owner.

The classic story of racing chicanery comes from Earnhardt pal Marshall Brooks. In a major race one of the cars won by making far fewer pit stops than the other drivers. They would be in for fuel and he would zoom past until the checkered flag dropped. Without hesitation, out came the protests. Regulations called for very specific size fuel tanks that all held exactly the same amount of fuel. Engines were meticulously fine-tuned to extract maximum mileage over the duration of the race. After the big finish, the inspectors gathered around the car parked out next to the track, convinced the gas tank was over the legal limit. They stripped out the tank and it was the correct size. They pried open the rocker panels, peered under the fenders, looked for hidden gas containers in air spaces. They found nothing. The driver/owner of the car asked if they were done and whether his car had passed their inspection. They said it had. With the empty gas tank still lying in the grass where it had been tossed, the driver got into the car and pressed the starter. The engine turned over, and the driver drove away back to the track garage past the gaping mouths and stares of the inspectors. The extra gas had been hidden in the hollow tubes of the roll cage that protects the driver. That innovation of shade tree culture continues to dog American stock car racing today.

Ralph was a regular customer of the Dayvaults since they had the only dynamometer—a mechanical device used for measuring the torque, force, or power from a spinning shaft whose speed is measured with a tachometer. Since horsepower is equal to torque multiplied by revolutions per minute (RPM), any torque increase results in a power increase at a given RPM level. This is why it is better to concentrate on improving torque instead of horsepower for the best performing engine.[9] Ralph tested all his cars at the Dayvaults' shop before he took them to the tracks. He also ordered the many parts he needed through the Dayvaults.

Frank Dayvault said, "It was cheap to race then. It wasn't a business. But Ralph was different, to Ralph it was a business. He was able to make a living at it when not many people could." Away from the track, he pretty much kept to himself except for a few close friends and stuck to his work.

"A lot of people called Ralph moody," said Ralph's wife, Martha. "But I think it was just that he didn't want to be disturbed when he was working. Dale got some of that from him."[10]

Martha is the anchor of the Earnhardt family. She's seen her husband, her son, and her grandson all become legends in stock car racing. Action on the track has been a constant in her life since she was 18 and Ralph was a national champion. When Dale was young, his father built him a go-cart that he ran in the field across from the house, and that later his own son, Dale Jr., inherited. It became a fixture in the Earnhardt family for four generations.

"Racing was just in his blood," Martha said. "He was just a normal boy growing up. He liked to cut up and tease his sisters' boyfriends and all the other things 'just boys' liked to do."[11]

In 1993, Martha's daughter Kathy was also racing and was a consistent winner at the Powder Puff Derby run at the Concord Speedway each year. Her daytime job at the time was supervisor at the Fieldcrest Cannon Mills Plant Four. One night, Martha endured having Ralph, Dale, Kathy, and a son-in-law all running in the same race at the Metrolina Track. "That just about gave me a heart attack," she remembers. "Racing is altogether different when you have children involved." In September 1993 Dale Jr. wrecked his car at a race in Myrtle Beach and he was very discouraged. Martha's motherly advice was simply, "Don't worry, your dad has torn up plenty of cars."[12]

Though Dale liked to build and take apart motors, his father never built a car for him. That's a chore he had to deal with himself. Ralph never encouraged or discouraged Dale's growing ambitions to become a race driver.

However, Ralph did like to show off his son's prowess with the low-slung go-cart and often asked Dale to demonstrate to visitors how he could run the little vehicle on the homemade track across the street. At age eight or nine he could spin the cart in donuts on the dirt surface, raising a cloud of dust. Later, during a celebration at the house after he won his first Winston Cup race at the track in Bristol, Tennessee, in 1979, he pulled out the old go-cart and sat down in it. To those assembled, he grinned and said, "This is where it all began."[13]

Ralph worked on his racers and custom jobs in his garage behind the house, a flat-roofed outbuilding with two bays and a workshop space. When he needed special parts made, he knew a source from his linthead days at the mill. Cannon Mills had a first class metal-working shop. Marshall Brooks, owner of Marshall Motor Company in Concord, North Carolina, who also needed parts for his racing motorcycles related:

> One of the guys that helped on those cars—his name was Petey—He worked at the mill in the machine shop and he'd make special parts for racers. That was called "government work." You did that before you did the mill work. So he'd make 10 of them to be sure there was enough. For example, we'd lighten the flywheel—we'd make a solid flywheel so you could go into the corner on a half-mile track and let off on it and it would just slow down just a little bit and cut back on the gas in the turn and it would just jump, whereas with the old heavy flywheel, the inertia, when you shut the motor going into the corner it would just stall. Of course everyone tried that but we had something that worked.

When he wasn't racing, Ralph often had his head under another racer's hood—often that of a competitor—who came to him to add speed to his mounts. One story Marshall Brooks tells is of the racer Grey London, who met Ralph in 1964 and asked him to jack up his Number 21 yellow Chevy at the 1412 Sedan Street shop. One day, London came into Earnhardt's shop and saw Ralph working on two identical engines, one for the yellow Chevy and another for one of London's rivals at the Concord racetrack.

Right away, London was struck by the small carburetor intake-opening cut for his car compared to the huge hole in the other engine. You didn't have to be an expert mechanic to know that the more air that could be sucked into the carburetor, the faster the car could go. London angrily pointed out the discrepancy to Ralph and stormed out of the shop. Later, he came back, still steaming, and Ralph looked up from his work.

"Something wrong, Bossman?" Ralph asked.

"Darn right there is," London shot back, firmly convinced Ralph was giving London's rival the edge in speed.

"Then let me tell you something," Earnhardt said. "That other fellow ordered a 389 Pontiac carburetor. He doesn't need that much fuel, but he told me what he wanted, so that's what I done. As for yours, well, Bossman, I built yours like I do mine. Trust me."

Running in the next race at Concord, London's car churned through the dirt twice as fast, and he was surprised that he could easily keep up with his rival. He set himself to put up with Ralph's good-natured ribbing about big and little holes for sucking air.[14]

All the drivers experimented in those days because they didn't have factory teams to do testing for them. When Grey London and Ralph were at Concord a few months later, they watched a driver named Chuck Piazza rumble out onto the dirt to run some test laps. On his hubs he had installed extra-wide tires. When he mashed the gas, his car just tore into the curves and zoomed out with seeming ease. London considered getting a set of those wide tires for his car.

Ralph said, "Nope."

London once again made a great protest that he "didn't stand a chance," and if they had some extra-wide tires, he wanted them on his car. On race day, London watched some boys rolling wide tires along the pits, but they went right past his car. And again he rounded on Earnhardt. "This is bull!"

"The traction you'll get is just fine," Earnhardt answered. "During the race, them wide tires will just slow him down. The narrower the tire, the better. Heck, I'd run a bicycle tire if I could."

The tires Earnhardt had planned to use were perfect for that track. He cut his own treads into the rubber depending on where he was running. London made one of his best finishes at Concord.

"I ate my hat," London admitted later. "He was right. Again."[15]

"In Ralph's shop," said Marshall Brooks, "you may come to visit, but he'd be working and you'd have to wait sometimes up to a half an hour. Then he'd hold a little conversation and go back to work. He was innovative. In those days, if you needed something, you made it."[16] Brooks knew Ralph and sponsored Dale at $75 a week when he began racing at age 17.

In Kannapolis, where racing and car worship were part hobby and part religion, Ralph Earnhardt had created a winning reputation that put food on the table and a roof over his family. Dale saw a place for himself in racing and spent every spare moment when his father was in his shop or at a local track making himself useful, listening and watching.

"I lived and breathed what he said," Dale remembered. "I just loved to hear him talk about racing. He was my hero and he was my role model."[17]

If anyone else expected pointers or idle chatter from Ralph Earnhardt, he went away disappointed. One such individual who was the motor-mouth-opposite of Ralph was a member of his circle named Torrance

Simpson, whom everyone called Jivie. He worked at Charlotte and the Lowe's Speedway for about 20 years.

Jivie had hung around the shop where his dad had been a mechanic for some 35 years. The kid had swept floors and run errands until he decided, in order to stay, that he'd have to learn a real skill, so he learned welding and became very good at it. Like Ralph, he also became obsessed with building cars from scratch. But it was hard to put up with Earnhardt's big silences.

"One day he called me and insisted that I come over," said Simpson. "I came up to his shop and Ralph comes out to talk. Then, somebody drove up in a car and he just put a zipper on his mouth. Once they drove up that was the end of our conversation. To this day I don't know what he wanted. I finally got in my car and said, 'See you later.' He said 'Okay.'"[18]

"Ralph let Dale learn on his own," said Frank Dayvault, "He helped him, but he wouldn't do the work for him."[19]

Dale's first paved-track race car, owned by his brothers-in-law, Ray and David Oliver, was a six-cylinder 1956 Ford Club Sedan sponsored by the Dayvaults. The number on the side was K-2 because that was how the track numbered their cars. There wasn't a lot of money to throw at the car so the paint job came from what was on the shelf in the shop at the time. The result was a pink body with a purple top. His first dirt race was at the Concord track owned by Henry Furr.

Ralph Deal, who supplied the Earnhardts with auto parts for 30 years and had the opportunity to see them both racing on the same track, said: "They raced together a few times at the Metrolina Fairgrounds in Charlotte and at the old Concord Speedway. I saw Ralph ride Dale's bumper and push him so he could learn how to handle it. Ralph would run as hard as he could until it blew. That served Dale, he was the same way. Ralph taught him how to bump, run and grind on the track. I remember he always wanted to be a winner."[20]

Earnhardt was much like his father who had left school after the sixth grade. Dale quit school at age 16, married Latane Brown when he was 17, and fathered a son, Kerry. Later, in 1970 he divorced Latane and married young Brenda Lorraine Gee and fathered two children, daughter Kelley on August 28, 1972, and Dale Earnhardt Jr. on October 10, 1974. Like most young people in the South at that time, work was scarce outside the textile mills, so Dale worked at a number of jobs, including a stint as a welder for his father-in-law, and called a few rental apartments, trailers, and a mill house home as he swapped paint on old dirt tracks and learned about racing and race cars. At this time, racing was his life and there was little room to spare for his wives and children. That single minded pursuit cost him dearly in his relationships.

## NOTES

1. Mike's NASCAR Page, http://www.mindspring.com/~mike.wicks/nascarhistory2.html.

2. "Red neck" comes from the red bandannas worn around the necks of Appalachian coal miners striking for better wages and conditions for their families in the 1920s.

3. Joe Menzer, *The Wildest Ride: A History of NASCAR* (New York: Simon & Schuster, 2001), pp. 148–149.

4. Ibid., p. 149.

5. Ken Willis, "Dale was destined for greatness," *Racing News*, www.news-journalonline.com/speed/special/Earnhardt/MEMMAIN.htm.

6. Ibid.

7. Ibid.

8. Ibid.

9. Dave Barnett, "Where the Rubber Meets the Road—Establishing a Base Line," Vintage MG Club of Southern California, http://www.vintagemg.com/ArticlePDFs/Tech107.pdf.

10. Ethel Sechler, "Champ's Mother is Very Proud of All Her Children," *Concord-Kannapolis Daily Independent* (Kannapolis, NC), October 3, 1993.

11. Ibid.

12. Ibid.

13. Ibid.

14. Grey London, "Following the Earnhardt Connection," *Concord-Kannapolis Daily Independent* (Kannapolis, NC).

15. Ibid.

16. Jennifer Woodford, "Dale Earnhardt: From the Pink K-2 to the Black #3," *All Race Magazine*, October 24, 2001, revised July 12, 2002.

17. Shawn A. Akers, "Dale Earnhardt's Daddy," *Concord-Kannapolis Independent Tribune*, May 17, 1997.

18. Willis, "Dale was destined for greatness."

19. Woodford, "Dale Earnhardt: From the Pink K-2 to the Black #3."

20. Ibid.

# Chapter 7

# TOUGH TIMES— KICKING IN THE DOOR

After a while Dale Earnhardt discovered some old Ford Falcons and selected one to be his new dirt race car. He fixed up the car in his spare time while supporting his family working as a welder for the Great Dane Trucking Company. The Falcon was a 1960s recession car built to a low price point, offering high gas mileage with its original 144-cubic-inch, 6-cylinder engine. It was an immediate success, giving families room for six and a low price for a lot of car. The racing model, of course, was stripped of the interior niceties, headlights removed and extra chrome stripped away from the sides.

Earnhardt paid his bills when he had the money. The family all rode around in old fixer-upper cars kept running with the same tools that pushed a continuous stream of race cars through the garage at the old Earnhardt family home on Sedan Avenue in Kannapolis. During this time, young Dale continued running in the dirt whenever he wasn't head-down in the bowels of some rank racer, working in the body shop, or learning from his dad about the mysteries of the internal combustion engine, transmissions, brakes, and the many critical parts that might influence the car's participation in the race.

When they absolutely had to step back from the scrap they were turning into cars, Dale and Ralph went hunting rabbits and squirrels and did some fishing. These pastimes along with a love of the outdoors stayed with Dale for the rest of his life. But there wasn't much time left for father and son to enjoy each other's company. On a warm evening, September 26, 1973, Ralph Earnhardt was working on one of his cars when he suffered a heart attack and died. His legacy left to Dale was hardly any money, a few old dirt cars, and a reputation in the racing world as a man with a heart of iron.

Ralph Earnhardt had begun racing in 1949 but had not raced professionally until 1953. Within three years, he was NASCAR Sportsman Champion. In that same year, 1956, he drove to 32 victories. Ralph raced in NASCAR seasons until 1968 and in his last year, he won the South Carolina Championship at the Greenville-Pickens Speedway. After leaving NASCAR, he raced closer to home to be near his family. He had winning points in 1969, 1970, 1971 and 1972 at the Concord track and at the Charlotte Speedworld. A versatile driver, at one time he held track championships at seven different speedways.

While Ralph had always driven what might be called a conservative race, going just hard enough to stay within striking distance of the lead and then going flat out for the win in the last laps, Dale, early on in his career, was a hard charger right from the green flag. His style was considerably less calculated than that of his dad which meant going for the front at all costs. He was no different from most of the starry-eyed southern boys who roared out of their pits and onto the tracks on weekend nights, but he was no car worshipper. He used cars and drove the wheels off them if need be. As he progressed from a one-man show with a pick-up crew of local kids to organized teams with sponsor money, he demanded the same level of preparation he had learned from Ralph. Using that criteria, he rose from the field to become one of the front-runners as his improving equipment matched his seat-of-the-pants skills.

The other part of his formula was the relationships he needed with his sponsor and crew. In these mid-life days of NASCAR, when the cars were still considered to be stock cars—performance versions of the showroom vehicles for sale to the public—sponsored by Detroit manufacturers, the car owners had a very personal relationship with their drivers. The best drivers, the earners, got the best cars, and Dale spent the 1970s bashing his way—literally—through dirt- track races and short-track races, often hand-hauling the heap of scrap that had been his car back to the Sedan Street garage. Cars he drove for other owners were treated no differently. But the tall, gangly kid with the mustache was always a crowd pleaser and almost always near the front when the wheels finally came off his ride or when he ended up smeared along the wall in a steaming wreck.

But all around him, times were changing. Racing was becoming a big business and no place for the faint of heart. While his little family lived in low-rent housing on what he earned and food stamps, Dale Earnhardt plugged away with single-minded determination.

For NASCAR, the 1960s were hard on some of the great names from that rowdy era of dirt racing. As new young drivers elbowed their way into the more prestigious races, many of the older drivers watched speeds go up and paved tracks require greater handling skills. Some got the word and quit driving to become car owners or found jobs as race broadcasters, in the shops, testing for manufacturers, and in other niches in the racing community.

NASCAR kept the changes coming, but while rules came and went and technology advanced, some things never changed. Southern stock car racing was a white man's sport. A few white women stepped up. But none of them were competitive and most failed to get enough sponsor money or a good-enough car. But African American men need not apply.

One driver, however, had the courage of his convictions and confidence in his talent not to be put off. Wendell Scott shoved back and became a legend. An independent driver and car owner on the Grand National Circuit was almost an oxymoron. Running a reasonably current model Grand National car took money, a crew, boxes of spare parts, a stack of tires, transportation, and a sponsor to sign checks and look after business. Being black didn't help one bit. His cars were hardly competitive with the manufacturer-supported Detroit machines, and his crew was mostly friends and family members—black mechanics no white driver would let near his car. The NASCAR rules said nothing about a driver having to be white to compete, so there was Scott, bringing in his rebuilt car wrapped around its rebuilt engine and hoping it would hold together for another 125 or 250 laps. The single edge he had on the other drivers when the flag dropped was his sheer talent. Wendell Scott was the Tiger Woods and Michael Jordan of his sport for natural ability behind a wheel. Driving in the South in the 1960s was hard enough facing the top racers—veterans and newcomers—but too many of his fellow competitors made it their job to put his car into the wall.

Often Scott traveled with his wife and growing family of kids. Blacks usually had their part of the grandstand separate from the whites. Stock car racing was a blue-collar sport and much of the fan base had grown up poor and uneducated. They did not want to share their sport with Negroes who were supposed to be a few rungs below them on the social ladder. Wendell had to save his comebacks to the racial taunts and garbage thrown from the stands for his performance on the track.

"If I'd have went through what Wendell Scott went through," said Junior Johnson, "I'd have never made it. And if I had to race the stuff he had, I wouldn't have lasted 10 races. His determination was thousand times more than what mine was."[1]

Scott was a whiskey tripper and got caught. A race promoter offered to bail him out if he would drive the promoter's car in a dirt-track race. Jumping at that opportunity, Scott discovered his true calling clawing through turns at high speed with no police chasing him and cash in his pocket when the checkered flag dropped. He was a novelty and many people came just to see a black man get wrecked. But it didn't work out that way. He drove in the dirt for 10 years, winning more than 120 races. He claimed the NASCAR Virginia State Sportsman Award. Scott moved into the Grand National Division in 1961.

His guts and skill kept him running GN cars for more than 12 years, logging 495 races with 147 top-10 finishes. He finished 20th or better in the points standing for nine straight seasons and kept in the top 10 for four in a row from 1966 to 1969. During those years, great drivers such as Bobby Allison, Buddy Baker, Ned Jarrett, and Cale Yarborough watched him go on by.

There were times when he had to defend himself. Working on a shoestring made any wreck hard to accept and stock car racing being what it is, fenders touch in tight quarters. It was hard to separate the accidental bumps from the deliberate ramming, but in one case, a driver named Jack Smith decided he was going to run Scott off the track. Every time Scott drew near Smith's car, "wump!" came a fender, or the scream of shearing metal as door panels banged together. And always it was Smith's car, edging closer, cutting in, bumping the rear. Finally in the middle of the race, running door handle to door handle, Smith began to shove Scott's car again. Then Smith froze. Across from him, Scott was driving with one hand on the steering wheel. In the other he held a .38 caliber revolver; the sun shown off the brass jacketed bullets in the cylinder as the muzzle pointed out the passenger side window. Smith's car slid off Scott's paintwork and disappeared to the rear into the jockeying cars roaring down the asphalt.

Not every moment ended well for Scott. On December 1, 1963, the flag dropped on a 200-lap race at the Jacksonville Speedway, a half-mile dirt track. Scott was at home and stormed into the lead, finally lapping the field twice. He hurtled toward the finish line, grimy with clay and victorious, but no checkered flag came out. He thought he had miscounted the laps. He took off again and the second time he passed the start-finish line, there was still no checkered flag. As he raced around for a third time, Buck Baker, running an entire mile behind him took the checkered flag.

Baker wheeled his car into victory lane, accepted the trophy, kissed the beauty queen, and accepted the crowd's cheering applause. Those NASCAR officials were not about to give the award to that black man in front of the white crowd. After the race when everyone had gone home, the error was corrected and a cheap wood trophy was cobbled together for

Scott and handed to him out of public view. Baker got to keep the gleaming Winner's Cup and settled for 2nd-place money.

Wendell Scott continued to race throughout the season, ending up 12th in the 1964 points standing with 8 top-5 showings and 20 top-10 showings in 56 races. He was a top competitor until 1972 when an accident at Talladega Speedway cut short his career leaving him in chronic pain. He died in 1990 of spinal cancer. In 1999, Wendell Scott was accepted into the Motorsports Hall of Fame—the only African American man to ever win a NASCAR race.

Herb Thomas, NASCAR's high-points leader in 1956, was ahead of Buck Baker going into a dirt-track race at the Cleveland County Fairgrounds in Shelby, North Carolina, when he tried to pass Buck for 2nd place. Alfred "Speedy" Thompson, one of the top drivers of the 1950s and Buck Baker's teammate clipped Herb's car and sent it spinning into the grandstand wall. With a shattering impact, the Thomas car caromed off the concrete into the path of a speeding gaggle of racers. His car was torn to bits and he was shipped to the Charlotte Memorial Hospital hanging on with a fractured skull and massive internal injuries with a less than 5 percent chance of pulling through.

After a three-month hospitalization, sliding in and out of a coma, he eventually survived. His driving skills never returned to his pre-accident capability and in 1962, he retired from racing.

The famous Flock brothers were flamboyant fixtures at southern stock car races. Fonty Flock never saw the 1960 season after his car spun out against the wall during the Southern 500 at Darlington and was struck by Bobby Myers whose car flipped end over end on down the track firing pieces in all directions. He died in the wreckage. Fonty Flock never raced again. Six months later, Bobby's brother Billy was racing in the Bowman-Gray Stadium in Winston-Salem, North Carolina, when he pulled his car off the track, switched off the engine, and died of a heart attack.

Speedy Thompson continued to race until April 2, 1972, when competing at the Metrolina Speedway in Charlotte, North Carolina, he died of a heart attack at age 45, one day before his birthday.

One of the biggest losses to the world of NASCAR racing occurred at the World 600 in Charlotte. Edward Glenn "Fireball" Roberts was the rock star of NASCAR at age 35 with 33 wins and 122 top-10 finishes. He earned the pole-start position 32 times in 206 races over his 15-year career. He had lived large and was already a racing legend. His "fireball" nickname came from a fast ball he hurled as a pitcher for the Zelwood Mud Hens, an American Legion baseball team.

By the time he was scheduled to race in the World 600 on May 24, 1964, Roberts was considering retirement. He had a spokesman deal for a major beer company for $50,000 a year and in 1963 had earned $73,000 from racing which gave him the 40 percent driver's cut amounting to about $30,000. Even though the race winnings were low, in 1963, they represented significant money. A $6,000 winning purse was more than the average worker's annual wage of $5,623, and a gallon of gas cost 25 cents. Roberts was ready to retire from the superspeedways.

At that time, NASCAR and a number of car owners had adopted fire retardant one-piece uniforms for drivers. Roberts, however, balked at the retardant chemicals impregnated in the cloth, saying they aggravated his asthma and made it hard for him to breathe during a race. His cotton coverall had no flame retardant applied to it. Not wanting to keep one of the big money draws to the sport out of the race, NASCAR honored the note from Roberts's doctor backing up his asthma claim. On the morning of the race, Roberts felt uneasy and his friends suggested he pack it in and not race that day.

"I can't do that," Roberts shot back. "All these people are here to see me race." Besides the fans, he was obligated to all of his sponsors as well. Finally, the bands played, the throaty growl of fast-rolling iron began circling the track, and with a scream of acceleration, the race was on. There are times when race drivers are just in the wrong place at the wrong time. Only seven laps had been clocked when Ned Jarrett and Junior Johnson touched. The rocketing parade flashing down the backstretch suddenly became a whirling, spinning calamity of cars and pieces of cars. From the middle of the dust and whistling debris erupted a pillar of black smoke belching into the sky. Trying to avoid Jarrett's and Junior's calamity, Roberts lost control and sailed into the wall, crushing his gas tank—still full of high-octane fuel—and exploding into all-engulfing flames. The car flipped over onto its back and the rear firewall gave way, allowing flaming gasoline to fill the cockpit.

Jarrett was out of his car that had rolled to a stop 30 feet away and ran across the track as Roberts flailed and screamed trying to squirm out of the blazing steel, "Help me! I'm on fire!" By the time he was dragged from the scorched wreck, he had suffered second- and third-degree burns over 80 percent of his body and was in terrible pain. Jarrett burned his hands badly trying to rescue his friend. Glenn "Fireball" Roberts lingered through the month of June but developed pneumonia and sepsis, finally succumbing on July 2, 1964.

His death added to the deaths of Indianapolis 500 drivers Eddie Sachs, driving a roadster, and Dave MacDonald, piloting Mickey Thompson's revolutionary rear-engine Sears Allstate Special in a fiery seven-car pile-up in the 1964 Indy race. This string of fiery deaths increased research by the racing industry into flame retardant, nonallergic chemicals. Public outcry and the press motivated testing to develop safe fuel cells and mandated carrying less fuel on board, and more pit stops were proposed. In addition, car owners began shifting from gasoline to less flammable methanol.

At the outset, NASCAR required drivers to take whatever clothing they were wearing for any race longer than a mile or more and dip it in fire retardant solution. Later, the DuPont Company developed Nomex flame-retardant cloth, which became the industry standard one-piece coverall. Flame retardant gloves and shoes were added to the kit, and death from fire became a greatly reduced threat.

Ned Jarrett retired in 1966 as did Junior Johnson, taking two more names from victory lane. Bill France was frantic to keep the star luster alive in NASCAR racing. In desperation he finally acknowledged wiser heads and reinstated Curtis Turner, who along with Tim Flock and Fireball Roberts had been bounced from NASCAR for advocating unionization of the drivers. Flock had retired; Roberts was dead; and Turner made his heartfelt return to NASCAR racing. His debut race was at the North Carolina Motor Speedway in Rockingham, a brand new 1.017-mile super-speedway, in a 500-mile race driving a brand new 1965 Ford. The all-new racetrack and Ford automobile added copy to the press reports when Turner won the race. He trounced Cale Yarborough, a new kid working his way up in the ranks, and veteran Marvin Panch for the victory.

Turner's party-hearty lifestyle had not changed since his enforced vacation from NASCAR racing, but now his body was 41 years old and creeping ruin was snuffing out those keen reflexes. He tried to rev up the winning formula a few times, but by 1966, he decided to quit racing and become a golfer. He became a fixture at many clubhouse lounges, hustling drinks instead of birdies. On October 4, 1970, he and golf professional Clarence King climbed into Turner's Aerocommander private plane and flew into the side of a Pennsylvania mountain, killing both of them. King was at the controls and Turner was dozing in the back, nursing a hangover.

Bill France had watched a stable of stars wink out during the 1960s just as the sport was gaining both momentum and legitimacy in racing circles. Stock car racing was still primarily a southern sport, but thanks to Detroit's explorations into sponsorship of cars and drivers, the influx of money and press interest had elevated the contests. The next generation of young drivers who had no shady background in whiskey tripping or jail time was making its presence felt among the top-10 finishers. And halfway through the '60s, with the Flocks gone and the Myers brothers gone, with Junior Johnson counting chickens on his farm, and the rest of the cigar-chomping, high-living old vets now backing car stables of their own, a new big name was needed. And it was Petty.

## NOTE

1. Joe Garner, *Speed, Guts and Glory* (New York: Warner Books, 2006), p. 194.

# Chapter 8

# TIE YOUR PENNANT TO A PETTY

Lee Petty had been in the trenches since the early 1950s. And like the Earnhardts, racing was the family business after steady jobs selling biscuits and owning a truck shop did not pan out. Unlike his fellow good old boys who enjoyed living high and fast cars even when they were not racing, Lee was more like Ralph Earnhardt, a family man. But while Ralph drove a conservative race—until someone tried to pass him or he wanted to make a hole between two cars where none existed—Lee took an all-around more aggressive approach. With wing nuts welded to his bodywork, he fastened steel plates to the sides of his Oldsmobile. These had the effect of shearing off odd bits of cars when competitors tried to shunt him off the track or when he felt the need to drive through a car rather than around it. Winning races put food on the table.

Young Richard Petty—also like Dale Earnhardt—earned his keep by helping Lee in the pits and in the workshop. One story has it that during a particularly hectic pit stop, while the crew changed tires and fueled up the Olds, Richard sprawled across the hood to swab the mud off the windshield. With a fresh load of gas and rubber aboard, Lee Petty looked over his left shoulder and floored the gas, swinging back out onto the track. When he looked straight ahead as the engine hammered away, he peered into the face of his boy, Richard. The lad had not scrambled off the hood in time and with no place to stop on the track, Lee motored around once with his son clinging white-knuckled to his race car, accepting the hoots, cheers, and joyful applause of the crowd.

Eventually, by the time the family was fully committed to stock car racing, Richard became his father's crew chief. In no time, as he turned

20 years old in 1958, Richard was behind the wheel and smashed into the wall courtesy of his dad. During his first Grand National–level race, Lee and Richard tried to occupy the same space on the track. Richard ended up sitting in a smoking wreck pressed to the concrete while Lee went on to win the race.

Bill France's celebrity mill seemed to have found a pair of crowd pleasers as father and son began racking up points and purses. In one race at the Jacksonville Speedway in November 1960, the younger Petty roared across the finish line as the checkered flag dropped—his first Grand National win. Coming in behind him was Lee Petty, who protested his son was a lap behind. The protest proved to be true. Lee Petty walked away with the $800 purse while Richard settled for 4th place and $275.

As the younger Petty learned the hard lessons of race driving, he also accumulated the wisdom of marketing his image. While all the hard chargers and veterans drove either Fords or Chevrolets, Petty was content to pilot a Plymouth for the Chrysler folks. No Ford fan could root for a Chevy driver if his main man dropped out. Petty's Number 43 Plymouth was always the fans' go-to car because they did not have to feel like deserters when their hero's Ford or Chevy fell out of a race for one reason or another. The Plymouth was underpowered compared to the other makes, so it had its best days on the shorter tracks where the more powerful cars had no place to build up their revs down the long straights.

Then, in 1964, Chrysler unveiled its 426-cubic-inch displacement hemi-engine they called King Kong. This wedge-head plant was released only for racing when running off a Holley four-barrel carburetor mounted on a dual-plane, high-rise intake manifold coupled to a four-speed manual gear-box, which gave the driver 0–60 miles per hour in 4.1 seconds. These engines used a hemispherical combustion chamber that allowed the two valves required for each cylinder to be angled, adding to the combustion-chamber space and allowing larger valves to be used. This improved the engine's airflow or breathing as the fuel ignited. The improvement resulted in more power. The engine was huge. Called an elephant by mechanics, it outsized any Ford or GM power plant.

When the first hemi-engine racer driven by Paul Goldsmith chugged out onto the Dayton 500 track in 1964 behind that monster and he mashed the gas pedal, Goldsmith qualified at 174.418 miles per hour—13 miles per hour faster than the previous record. The big King Kong Plymouth exploded onto the racing scene carrying Petty to the checkered flag in that race and 37 top-five finishes in his next 61 starts.

After winning the 1964 Grand National Championship, Richard Petty could taste the upcoming 1965 season championship. Bill France suddenly pulled the plug and outlawed the King Kong engine from NASCAR racing. He claimed that it was not a "readily available stock engine" sold to the public. It violated the stock car concept. Petty Enterprises pulled out of NASCAR in a fury. Chrysler pulled their support and cars from NASCAR's 1965 season. In an attempt to match the Plymouth hemi-engine, Ford and Chevrolet had created overhead camshaft engines that NASCAR also rejected. Chevrolet also withdrew their cars in protest.

Challenging Bill France's apparently high-handed disqualification, Richard Petty stuffed a 426 King Kong hemi into a custom drag racer, the Super Stock Barracuda named Outlawed, and campaigned around the American Hot Rod Association's southern drag tracks for $1,000 in appearance money. One night, however, Petty lost control of the Barracuda and plowed into the stands, killing an eight-year-old boy and injuring many fans. Deeply moved over the incident, he withdrew from all racing. He eventually rejoined the NASCAR circuit in 1966 racing more conventional Plymouths—and won the Daytona 500 for a second time, the first driver to do so. Bill France had also shifted his position slightly, allowing the new hot-engine cars to race on tracks of a mile or less in length.

*Ralph Earnhardt lived in this home and worked in the garage out back. Young Dale grew up here and his mother, Martha, still lives on the premises. Dale played in his home-built go-cart in the lot across the street and all the children visited regularly.*

*Ralph Earnhardt, 75, starts to spin out as he attempts to pass Emanuel Zervakis, 20, on the first turn of the Darlington International Raceway during the Rebel 300 at Darlington, South Carolina, May 14, 1962. The other drivers are Johnny Allen, 47, and Ned Jarrett, 11. AP Photo/Spencer Jones.*

This fire suit was worn by Dale Earnhardt during his 1981 Winston Cup victory when he was driving for Rod Osterlund. The suit is flame retardant and gives sponsors a walking billboard for their logos. It is on display at the Dale Earnhardt Enterprises Inc. Museum.

Called the Garage Mahal by locals, this complex is situated alongside a two-lane country road in Mooresville, North Carolina. There is no sign designating the property; visitors just have to know what the complex represents. Inside is a shrine to Earnhardt's memory. He was one of the finest NASCAR drivers and earned his fans' respect.

Dale Earnhardt, left, and his son, Dale Earnhardt Jr., right, from Kannapolis, North Carolina, watch from the pit area at the Daytona International Speedway as their GTS class Corvette powers through the grandstand straightaway, Thursday, February 1, 2001, in Daytona Beach, Florida. The Earnhardts, of NASCAR fame, will join two others driving the Corvette in Saturday's Rolex 24 Hour Race at Daytona. AP Photo/ Amy Conn.

Dale Earnhardt leans on the hood of his backup Chevrolet while crew members change out an engine Friday afternoon, February 9, 2001, at the Daytona International Speedway in Daytona Beach, Florida. AP Photo/Chris O'Meara.

NASCAR driver Dale Earnhardt Jr. in the AMP Energy/National Guard car as teams prepare for the Daytona 500 auto race Sunday, February 8, 2009, in Daytona Beach. AP Photo/J Pat Carter.

Nine-foot-tall bronze statue on a marble pedestal in the center of the Earnhardt Square Memorial in downtown Kannapolis, North Carolina. This is the way town folks knew him, as a regular guy wearing jeans and boots, driving his pickup truck, rather than as the millionaire racing driver.

This granite memorial is located in the circle of symbolic elements that make up the square containing the Earnhardt statue in the center of downtown Kannapolis, North Carolina. Symbolism from his career—the number three that was on his winning car for many years, the number seven pointing to his seven NASCAR championships, and the circular walk around his statue, symbolizing the many tracks he raced upon.

# Chapter 9

# GROWTH PAINS—
# PUSHING THE LIMIT

By the middle of the 1960s, there was a constant wrangle going on between the three main Detroit manufacturers. Big money was calling the tune and Ford, Chevrolet, and Chrysler had seen the effect winning cars had on their sales. Advertising budgets climbed, touting the success of the latest winning combination. Any car that could blast along all day at 200 miles per hour could certainly handle conditions on Route 66 or even the new turnpikes and expressways winding across the face of the country. Tires that skidded, drifted, careened, and scoured off their treads over a 500-mile race were sure good enough for trips to the store in Grandpa's Chevrolet Bel Air. Whatever it took to roll into victory lane became the rule of the day.

Doctoring cars was nothing new. In the early dirt-track days, shade tree mechanics who had a gift for shaving off weight and pumping up horsepower found a waiting line of customers on Monday mornings. Back then in the '40s and '50s, inspections were casual at best. By the late 1960s, Grand National inspectors had seen it all. Lightweight aluminum hoods were yanked off cars. Side panels thinned by immersion in acid were dented with thumb pressure. Braces and interior attachment beams were drilled with holes or skeletonized. Weight was the enemy.

The whole point of stock car racing in Bill France's mind was running cars that looked like cars on the showroom floor. Brand competition extended beyond the track as American drivers identified their assembly line cars with the racers that boomed around tracks on weekends across the country. The manufacturers, however, sank money into special design teams the dreamed up supercars that resembled nothing rolling down Main Street on a grocery-shopping Saturday afternoon.

Those bell ringers that arrived in 1969–70 were among the scariest racing machines ever developed. These supercars cut a swath through NASCAR competition until "homologation" shut them down. This word comes from the Greek meaning "to agree" which, in English is synonymous with "accreditation," or agreeing with a defined set of rules and regulations.

In racing series that are production-based (that is, the vehicles entered in the series are based on production vehicles for sale to the public), homologation entails not only compliance with racing series technical guidelines (for example, engine displacement, chassis construction, suspension design, and such), but it often includes minimum levels of sales to ensure that vehicles are not designed and produced solely for racing in that series. Since such vehicles are primarily intended for the racetrack, use on public roadways is generally a secondary design consideration, except as required to meet government regulations.

This hard-line set of regulations was cobbled together during the 1969–70 seasons, but not before the supercars swept beneath the checkered flag with monotonous regularity. The Ford Motor Company took its Torino two-door fastback sedan and turned it into the Torino Talladega in its Atlanta, Georgia, plant in 1969. To better slice through the air, the front end was made more sleek by replacing the grille and lights with a six-inch longer nose that had a wedge-shaped front end and a front bumper that was fashioned from a rear bumper fitted flush with the molded nose. On the sides, the rocker panels were rolled under for a lower ground clearance allowed by NASCAR rules, but this was impractical for regular road use.

The Talladega, built specifically for racing, crammed a Ford Boss 429-cubic-inch engine under the hood after the Ford 427 had been banned by NASCAR. Production models of the car had a 428 Cobra Jet power plant, which was still powerful, but not quite up to racing specs. While inspectors were giving Ford engineers a hard time over the 427, the 429 Boss had been stuffed into Ford Mustang Boss 429s. This find-the-engine shell game resulted in production of 754 Ford Talladegas, some of which found their way onto the street.

The sleek and subtle Ford Talladega piloted by a number of drivers scooped up 29 Grand National titles in 1969, including the 1969 championship driven by David Pearson, an up-and-coming rival for Richard Petty. To call the Talladega subtle is to use a relative term compared to the competition fielded by Plymouth and Dodge in that short but exciting era of the aerobirds.

The Dodge Charger 500 found itself being regularly trounced by the Talladega bomb, so Dodge engineers came back hard with the Dodge Charger Daytona for the 1970 season. This hot and beautiful *bolide* was wheeled out in the summer of 1969, the first of the revolutionary aerocars. Immediately recognizable by its 23-inch wing-tail stabilizer growing from its rear deck, a NASA-designed nose-cone aerodynamic replacement for its standard grill and a flush rear window area, the Daytona looked fast just standing still. Heavy-duty brakes and suspension supported the 440-cubic-inch Magnum engine with a 426 CID hemi-engine available in 70 of the 503 Dodge Daytonas built specifically for NASCAR racing.

Not just a pretty face, the Dodge Charger Daytona won its very first race, the Talladega 500, thumbing its nose at its rival Ford Torino Talladega. In that same year, Buddy Baker floored the gas and took the Chrysler Engineering Dodge Charger Daytona past the 200-mile-per-hour mark at Talladega on March 24, 1970, to set a NASCAR speed record. This car's main competition also carried the Chrysler crest, the Plymouth Superbird.

Another set of hot wheels designed for the NASCAR superspeedways and Grand National Competition, the Superbird took its name from its basic platform, the Plymouth Roadrunner. Along with the Dodge Charger Daytona, the car was one of the first to be designed using computer data gathered from wind-tunnel testing. It also employed the nose-cone front end and retractable headlights that tacked on 19 inches to the Roadrunner's stock front end. That same rear wing—called a spoiler—rose from the rear deck into less disturbed air flow, helping plant the rear tires firmly on the asphalt as speeds climbed. Air scoops that faced to the rear were used to free air trapped in the wheel wells. With a curious eye to practicality in this unique racing machine, another reason for the wing's height was to allow the trunk lid to open with no obstruction. No one bothered to mention what they planned to carry in the trunk while humping along at 200 miles per hour on a closed race course. It was a nod to future public sales of a less dangerous version.

Under the hood, the Superbird was stuffed with one of three engine options: a blazing 426 CID Hemi, the 440 CID Super Commando with a four-barrel carburetor or a pumped-up 440 CID Super Commando Six Barrel—called the 440 Sixpack—offering three two-barrel Holley carburetors producing 390 horsepower. The Superbird lured Richard Petty back to Chrysler for the 1970 season from his 1968 defection to Ford. He ran against the Ford Torino Talladega in many races that year, winning eight and placing high in the top 10 in many others.

Like the Ford Torino Talladega and Dodge Charger Daytona, Plymouth's Superbird fell afoul of NASCAR's homologation rules stating that for a car to be able to race on NASCAR tracks, it must be available to the general public "in sufficient numbers." This definition raised the availability number from 500 examples to one car for every two dealers in the United States. To meet that requirement, Plymouth would have had to build 1,920 Superbirds. Like its aerodynamic sisters, the Plymouth version of the aerocar was only produced through the 1970 season.

# Chapter 10

# IRONHEAD

The goal of racing is clear. When the checkered flag falls you are in front, or somewhere in the back.

*—Paul Newman, race driver*

The 1970s were tumultuous years of big losses and big wins for young Dale Earnhardt. He lost his father and mentor, Ralph, in 1973, changed wives three times, and started a family. During all that time, he beat his head against a career he so desperately wanted to master.

Marshall Brooks, who owned Docs Cycle Center and sponsored motorcycle races, bought a Chevrolet Chevelle from car owner Harry Gant and gave it to Dale to race. He said:

> There was a place called Lee's Sandwich Shop. Dirt trackers ate there. They worked as pipe fitters and plumbers. They ran out of Concord and Hickory. Everyone raced Friday nights and the racers worked at their jobs on Monday nights so they would have Thursdays off from the mill to prepare their cars. Come Friday, the grandstands were full. We were sitting there one night in Lee's and one of the guys said, "We need a race car." They told me, "You buy the car, we'll build and maintain it." I said, "You do the racing, I'll do the drinking." I don't mean this with any unkindness, but you'll find a lot of people who say they'll do anything to get into racing, but racing cost Dale two wives. He was so involved nothing else mattered. He's the first person I've ever seen, or known personally that even if it didn't

pay anything to race, if he had the money to race a vehicle, he'd race for nothing.

Once Dale asked me if I wanted to go to Hickory with him. So I went; the brothers were with him. He asked me to ride with him in the Chevelle while he turned laps around the track. I sat on the floor of the Chevelle—there was no passenger seat or back seat. They were stripped out to reduce weight. Dale said, "I'll head to the wall in turn three." It looked like he would hit the wall—he just missed it. He did that five times.[1]

Grand Prix drivers in Europe and the United States, the cream of race drivers in the world, call that kind of performance "ten-tenths driving." Truly gifted drivers estimate a corner can be taken at 97 miles per hour. They will go into that corner and round its apex at exactly 97 miles per hour. At 95–96 miles per hour they will lose time against a faster driver on every lap. At 98 miles per hour, the car will break loose its traction and spin off the track.[2] Dale Earnhardt had the feel for his car to be able to judge the degree of entry into a corner to the maximum ability to feel the four contact points of the tires on the track. And he had the concentration to do it on every circuit. While American stock cars are far less complex than Grand Prix Formula One or Indianapolis open-wheel racers, their principles are the same regarding speed versus traction—the great equalizers.

Earnhardt's thirst for information did not stop with the circle of his friends in and around Kannapolis and Concord. He often made pilgrimages to Junior Johnson's Ronda race shop where Bob Yates worked. He would hang out and ask questions. A new dynamometer had arrived and he wanted to run some parts on it. Sometimes he came up with Ralph, who took away bent shocks to straighten them at the Earnhardt garage. Dale also collected a share of used parts from the Junior Johnson shop for his own needs.

"We was poor," says Bob Yates, "but they didn't have nothing. Ralph came around and got all the broken parts, then take them home and fix what he could. That's why I was never jealous of Dale when he did well later. They didn't have anything to start with."[3]

"He had a natural feel for the car," Brooks said. "He had it in the seat of his pants. He could feel when the car was just short of getting loose. That happens fast on asphalt. He also sat differently from most drivers in the car. He sort of laid back and leaned over against the side. It's how he drove on dirt tracks."[4]

On a dirt track in Wilson, North Carolina, Dale was driving his father-in-law's Number 17 dirt car and had grabbed the lead in the 200-lap race. Suddenly, he spun out, but instead of letting up on the gas, he just dropped a gear and kept on plowing ahead once he straightened out. Fortunately, a yellow flag came out and he rolled into the pits. The crew slammed on two right side tires and spilled about seven gallons of gas in the tank, and he rolled back out into the race. Four laps later the Number 17 car was back in the lead once again where it stayed.

"He was hard-headed—a bullhead," says Jivie Simpson, "but he could drive a race car."[5]

When Dale wasn't racing, or building engines, or prowling around the various race shops, he hung out at a service station called Sandy Ridge on Route 153. It was a regular place for locals to drink a beer, maybe toss a few horseshoes and talk about car racing. In his early dirt-track days, he was a regular drop-in. Everybody in town knew him, but later, as the NASCAR points began to accumulate and he started showing up in the newspapers holding trophies, he couldn't just stop in with his pals anymore or there would be a mob scene.[6]

As he raced on dirt and pavement when he could get a ride, his wild-child attitude often came to the surface. He would come home angry to the core about something that happened during the race: getting a bump, or being squeezed out, cut off, or deliberately spun by another driver. He could never imagine doing such things even though a reality check showed the opposite.

Dale and Brenda soon had a son, Dale Jr., born in 1974. That same year Dale switched from dirt racing to asphalt. He picked up a used race car and drove in local races as part of the old Sportsman division which later became the Busch Circuit. He made his debut on the Winston Cup Circuit at the Charlotte Motor Speedway, driving in the Charlotte 600 on Memorial Day 1975. He drove car Number Eight—his Dad's number—a Dodge belonging to Ed Negre and his mechanic son, Norman. Earnhardt started in 33rd place, finished at 22nd place in the race, and pocketed $2,425. He was banging his way into the big time, rough as a cob and wrecking often, but he was on his way. His next race was taking over Johnny Ray's ride—Ray had a very brief NASCAR career—and crashed it. Dale's debut on full-time asphalt was hardly a success and economics drove him back to dirt-track racing where he could still win.

In 1978, Dale came back to help out Humpy Wheeler and fill in for the eventually famous African American driver Willy T. Ribbs at the '78 World 600 after Ribbs was arrested for evading police and driving down a street the wrong way. He had skipped two practice sessions. Ribbs built his

25-year career where Wendell Scott had left off. He was the first African American to qualify and compete in the Indianapolis 500. He won the Formula Ford Dunlop Championship in Europe and won two Driver of the Year awards while driving for race champions Dan Gurney, Jack Roush, and Derek Walker. Ribbs was the first African American to compete in the CART/Indy Championship in partnership with Bill Cosby and the first and only African American to test for the Formula One Grand Prix team in Estroil, Portugal. And in the United States, he became the first African American to compete in NASCAR's Winston Cup Series. Ribbs raced well into the 1990s and became the winningest African American driver of all time.

Dale drove for three more years making eight Winston Cup starts. The last race of that 1978 season was driving Rod Osterlund's second car in the Dixie 500 at Atlanta. He finished 4th, one spot behind Osterlund's regular driver, Dave Marcus. Following that race, Dave quit the team to start his own operation.

Humpy Wheeler became friends with Dale and campaigned for Dale to drive the Number 98 car owned by Rod Osterlund. Aware of Earnhardt's car breaking style, Osterlund was reluctant, but he was looking for a winner and gave the new kid a break, paying Dale $5,000. Dale proceeded to pilot the Number 98 car into 2nd place at Charlotte behind the champion, Bobby Allison. Following that race, Dale became Osterlund's driver.

As a car owner, Osterlund had started his team in 1977. He managed 201 starts until he called it quits in 1991. He gave opportunities to many long-shot racers. In 1980 he gave a ride to Grand Prix Formula One and sports car driver Dan Gurney, which turned out to be the racer's last run as a driver. From there Gurney had turned his talents to car design and his Eagles became legends in the open-wheel circuits. In that same year, a 42-year-old lady slid into an Osterlund car, her 33rd start in NASCAR racing. Janet Guthrie had already finished three starts as the first woman to compete in the Indianapolis 500 race.

One thing Osterlund recognized was Earnhardt's ragged style. Having grown up dirt-tracking, he drove every race like he was still driving on red clay. Osterlund wanted to enter cars at Watkins Glen in New York. To perform there, Dale had to smooth out his car handling. There was only one place that taught that level of car handling backed up by a professional driver whom everyone respected. Dale headed west to Ontario, California, and the tender mercies of Bob Bondurant's School of High Performance Driving.

The idea of a high-performance driving school is primarily a European idea. It's much harder to get a driving license in Europe and especially in countries such as Germany, where speed limits are virtually nonexistent on the *Autobahnen*. In the United States, teenagers take a few courses in high school, a simple road test, and they are eligible to sit behind the wheel of a 300-horsepower family sedan feeling pretty good about their skills. If they are very lucky, they will be involved in a near-miss, which will sober them considerably and demonstrate the explosive power in even the most modest two-door automobile. Race drivers are no less cocky about their abilities until they have been pried out of a wreck a few times, saved by as much dumb luck as skill.

Bob Bondurant's school teaches at two levels, accident avoidance and defensive driving for street motorists, and the high-performance precision driving needed by *pilotes*, who control the fastest automobiles in the world over closed courses. Graduates include: Al Unser Jr., Rick Mears, Chip Ganassi, Scott Sharp, Casey Mears, Bill Elliott, Dale Earnhardt, Dale Earnhardt Jr., Dan Gurney, Stirling Moss, Tony Stewart, Jeff Gordon, Brett Bodine, Chris Kneifel, Robbie Buhl, Robby Gordon, Tommy Kendall, John Andretti and such celebrities as Paul Newman, James Garner, Dick Smothers, Tim Allen, Tom Cruise, William Shatner, Walter Payton, Terrell Owens, Candice Bergen, Clint Eastwood, Gene Hackman, and many others.[7]

Bonderant began racing in 1959 as the top Corvette driver in the United States. Later he joined up with Carol Shelby, who had shocked the world with the Cobra and helped the car designer win the World Manufacturing Championship in 1965. Bondurant drove Formula One cars: American Eagles, British BRMs, and Italian Ferraris. At LeMans in June 1967, the steering broke at 150 miles per hour, flipping him 10 times on down the track. Surviving multiple compound fractures in both feet, he survived and recovered to run in long-distance marathons.

Although Dale passed through Bondurant's course in 1979, Watkins Glen went financially bust in 1981. It reopened in 1983, but it would be up to Dale Earnhardt Jr. to win there in the 1990s. Dale Jr. also attended Bondurant's school.

In his first season of full-time Grand National racing, Earnhardt blazed through 1979, winning his first Winston Cup at the short Bristol track after only 16 starts piloting Osterlund's Chevrolets. He went on to become the fastest qualifier at Riverside to win his first pole-position start and finished the season with 11 top-five finishes. His record beat out Harry Gant, Terry Labonte, and Joe Millikan in a close battle for Rookie of the Year. He had proved himself to be a tough and winning competitor as NASCAR barreled out of the 1970s and into a rapidly changing decade of the '80s.

## NOTES

1. Marshall Brooks, interview with the author, Concord, NC, October 16, 2008.

2. Ken Purdy, *Ken Purdy's Book of Automobiles* (New York: Playboy Press, 1972), p. 10.

3. Ken Willis, "Dale Was Destined for Greatness," *Racing News.* www.news-journalonline.com/speed/special/Earnhardt/MEMMAIN.htm.

4. Brooks, interview with the author.

5. Concord-Kannapolis Independent Tribune, www.newsjournalonline.com/speed/special/earnhardts/memmain.htm.

6. Brooks, interview with the author.

7. D. Brian Smith, "Bob Bondurant School of Performance Driving: In The Racer's Seat," *Kit Kar*, http://www.kitcarmag.com/eventcoverage/0807kc_bonduraunt_driving_school/index.html.

# Chapter 11

# A VOLATILE TIME FOR NASCAR

The aerocars of the 1969–70 season had been crowd pleasers for their aerodynamic look, their blade-like spoilers and the raw power of the 400-cubic-inch engines. But they had not been stock cars available to the public in dealer showrooms. They had violated Bill France's dictum of pure stock cars that kept the myth alive for the public that their cars in the parking lot had some kinship to the actual racers on the track.

But the crowd had been pleased by the power and speed. In 1968, France upped the ante by supporting a new fast superspeedway in Talladega, Alabama, a 2.66-mile paved ovoid with 18 degrees of banking in the curves and 4,000-foot straights. It was a 200-mile-per-hour track if anybody had the guts to try.

The drivers—the best ones—had the guts, but there were concerns about safety. Those concerns and a building need for better amenities in the garages, crew facilities, and other long ignored requests raised that spectre of a drivers' union once again. Just before the Yankee 600 race at Ann Arbor, Michigan, in August 1969, some of the top drivers in NASCAR met, including Richard Petty, Bobby Allison, Donnie Allison, Lee Roy, Cale Yarborough, Buddy Baker, and David Pearson, to discuss the problem. From this meeting came the Professional Drivers Association or PDA.

One of the major differences between this organization and the one championed by Curtis Turner back in 1961 was the lack of any affiliation with the Teamsters, who were allegedly controlled by the mob. Despite that exception, Bill France refused to have anything to do with the PDA or even acknowledge its existence. He simply referred to the drivers as "that bunch."[1]

The one really significant hold-out against the PDA was Bobby Isaac, an old pal of Ralph Earnhardt's and Bill France's. For his loyalty, he received from Bill a gold Rolex watch engraved with "Winners don't quit and quitters don't win" on the back.

When it came to the safety concerns about Talladega, that bunch had a lot to say about running a 500-mile race at top speed on a two-mile track considering the wear on tires. France, of course, pooh-poohed their worries. To really trump the PDA, France set up a stunt for the press. He pulled on a helmet, buckled into a Holman-Moody Ford and rolled out onto the Talladega track. This 59-year-old man who had no business in a high-speed modern racer began cranking off laps, slowly at first and then screaming around the asphalt. His best lap was turned at 176 miles per hour. When he rolled back into the pits, he felt he had vindicated the track and ability of the cars to reach high speeds.

Following his coup, France added insult by asking Bobby Allison if he could join the PDA. He had no desire to return to racing, but from the inside, he might cause all sorts of mischief. Ignoring the protests of the PDA, France pushed ahead with the inaugural Talladega 500-mile race.

Car testing began and teams sent their vehicles out onto the two-mile tri-oval. This was a big moment for Bill France. From dirt tracks in the boondocks and counting out sweat-damp dollars from a coffee can after cow-pasture races in Podunkville he now watched the cream of manufacturers' stock cars boom out of the pits, gear up onto the front straight, sail into the banked turn, and rocket down the backstretch. He had been there. He knew the thrill of the concrete wall flying by, the blur of the seats, the heat blasting back from the churning mill under the hood, the jitter of the steering wheel on the banking, and the slight lift as the car seemed on the edge of control. He had his triumph thundering down out of turn four and blasting past the grandstands. Bobby Allison led the way with a searing lap at 197 miles per hour.

And then the tires began to shred. Some sets of tires lasted only three laps. The low-slung cars began bottoming out, pounding the track with their undersides, sending bone-jarring jolts up the steering wheel shafts, bouncing feet off the pedals. The August heat on the asphalt, coupled with the unrelenting heat buildup from the constant high speed was blistering the rubber, baring the chord, disintegrating the tires. Car after car waddled back into the pits with junk hanging from its hubs.

The PDA forced a meeting with Bill France asking that the race be postponed. France blustered that the track was safe at 170 miles per hour—he'd demonstrated that. Petty countered that actual laps by the expert drivers easily clipped along at 190 miles per hour. The idea of running the race at less than flat out seemed ridiculous. Drivers holding back while others were at full speed became dangerous obstacles. The result would be similar to European rallies where Ferraris raced alongside Volkswagens in different classes on the same course at the same time—but at 170–190 miles per hour.

France dug in his heels and the meeting was over. The race would happen on the following day. That evening as the drivers hoped for some sort of compromise, the loudspeaker in the garage area informed the drivers who would not be racing to please remove their cars from the garage area. In a few minutes, 32 drivers, led by Richard Petty, had rolled their cars back onto trailers and into semitrucks to exit the premises. The race did come off the next day minus the big name drivers, but France offered fans a free race at the next NASCAR event at Talladega or Daytona, which seemed reasonable to the 65,000 that showed up—far below the 100,000 that had been expected.

On top of the rebuke to the PDA drivers, France added a good-faith pledge to the entry forms for future races, two paragraphs that obligated the cars and drivers to run once they had qualified. The incident polarized the racing community with some old veterans who had driven for peanuts on the old nasty dirt tracks coming down on the young drivers for making too much money and gaining fame too fast to appreciate what they had. Other race organizations beat up on France for being tyrannical and obstinate in his views.

France just folded his arms and pointed to the inaugural Talladega 500 race won by Richard Brickhouse whose pole speed was 196 miles per hour and average speed was 153 miles per hour. At the last minute, Goodyear had shipped in a load of tires that stayed in one piece for the 500-mile grind. The race had come off without a single accident due to tire failure. France also had allies among the car manufacturers. Petty was pressured by Chrysler, for whom he drove, to sign the new pledge forms as they were written. The legality of the forms was legally iron-clad and implied that NASCAR could squeeze the car owners to put alternate drivers into the cars to replace those who balked. France had won, and one by one the big stars of racing folded their hands and capitulated.

The 1970s brought one other huge change in NASCAR's regulations. The use of restrictor plates was announced at both the Daytona International Speedway and Talladega Superspeedway. The restrictor plate is a square of metal drilled with four holes, each about the size of a quarter. It fits on the engine between the air filter and carburetor and the air intake holes that feed the cylinders with the air-gas mixture to be ignited by the spark plugs. The restrictor holes are smaller than the regular holes drilled for this purpose and thereby restrict both the amount of air mixing with the gas and also the speed of the engine. With the plates in place, the cars cannot attain the 190-mile-per-hour speeds possible on these two tracks.

In effect, Bill France had 200-mile-per-hour tracks built and sanctioned and then prevented the cars from ever reaching that speed in the cause of safety. Another reason for the plates was to level the playing field. NASCAR wanted the teams with smaller budgets to be able to race their 358-cubic-inch engines against the better-financed shops running 427-cubic-inch motors. The restrictor plates were placed on the bigger engines to allow fair competition. The plates were phased out in 1974 as NASCAR mandated the 358-cubic-inch engine as the standard.

However, in 1987 at the Winston 500, Bobby Allison blew a tire at high speed on the Talladega tri-oval and spun his Buick LeSabre off the track, just barely saved by new high fencing from flying into the grandstands, and injured several fans. The restrictor plates came out once again.

To further level the playing field and ensure against any shenanigans by crew chiefs before the race, a NASCAR-authorized official asked team members to select the plates randomly from a pile during inspection and then, as though exhibiting a prize trout at a fish market, the official displayed the plate over his head for all to see. The holes were measured and the plate was placed on the engine. After the engine was given a special NASCAR seal, it was then closed up and remained in that condition through the race.

One of the drivers' complaints about the plates was that with every engine performing the same way, the cars tended to "pack up," to form a knot of close-packed jostling racers that caused more than average contact between the cars. This contact often resulted in spin-outs and bumping that resulted in cars kissing the wall at high speeds. It was harder for drivers to break away from the pack, and the pack itself formed a mass that caused a sort of draft that sucked the cars along at greater speed.

Restrictor plates were just the tip of the iceberg when it came to NASCAR mandating speed and design regulations to modify the sport depending on which way the profit wind was blowing. Along about this time in 1971, money was flowing into NASCAR at a pretty good clip, but while some of it was from auto-related industries: spark plugs, tires, gasoline additives, and so forth, the big sponsors were the Detroit manufacturers. The only problem with sacks of money coming from these automakers was everyone got used to the good life. As long as the Chevrolets, Fords, Dodges, Plymouths, and other GM brands circled the tracks, fan loyalty helped sell cars. The drivers, on the other hand, also had to be loyal to their make of car and sometimes the car and/or the crew were not up to the task of keeping that driver in the winner's circle.

Difficulties came with the homogenizing of the engine, gas capacity, tires, and so forth to specific requirements. This practice made the make or model of car virtually irrelevant. Fan loyalty began shifting to the drivers. Another nagging problem with having a long season of races fueled by automaker sponsorships was their volatility. For one reason or another during the late 1960s and 1970s, automakers saw fit to pull their cars from the racing circuit. Stability was needed.

The tobacco companies were kicked off television in 1971 for giving laboratory mice deep hacking coughs and causing cancer in adult humans. The result was vast advertising budgets with nowhere to spend them. Car owners suggested to corporations such as R. J. Reynolds that they speak to Bill France and buy into American stock car racing. They had already gotten their toes wet in the Winston Golden State race at California's Riverside track. France suggested the Grand National race series could use a serious sponsor and Reynolds leaped at the idea with the Winston Cup Grand National Championship that was shortened later to the Winston Cup Series. Now the drivers had a real pot of gold waiting at the end of the season's point standings.

Another phenomenon that emerged in the 1970s was television. Before then, watching a stock car race was as exciting as watching paint dry. The screens were small; most were black and white; and you couldn't really see anything. Open-wheel racing such as the Indianapolis 500 allowed TV viewers to see the driver, and the cars seemed so much more dangerous than the souped-up family sedans going around and around in circles. Even dirt-track midget races drew TV audiences as did nighttime demolition derbies.

ABC Sports showed portions of the 1962 Daytona 500, but it wasn't until April 10, 1971, that ABC broadcast the first flag-to-flag NASCAR race, the Greenville 200 from the Greenville-Pickens half-mile speedway in South Carolina. Considerable advance planning went into the show, because ABC needed a race that started and finished within 30 minutes. The field of cars was trimmed down to 26 from 30 racers to reduce the chance for clock-eating yellow caution flags that come out and slow the race down while debris is picked up off the track or oil slicks are covered. The small track was littered with scaffolding while the studio techs piping the feed to New York had to set up shop in a track toilet.

One of the big fears of television broadcasting was the audience might remain at home because the race was on TV. That fear proved groundless as the Greenville-Pickens grandstands filled to capacity. The cars were sent out circling the track when *Wide World of Sports* went on the air. A signal was fed to the starter and he brought down the green flag. With a roar the race thundered into thousands of homes that Saturday afternoon and began another new era in NASCAR and sports broadcasting history. One hour and sixteen minutes later, Bobby Isaac blew across the finish line, the winner. His team took home $20,000 thanks to the additional revenue from ABC—a record prize for a NASCAR 100-mile race.

ABC *Wide World of Sports* with sportscaster Chris Economaki eventually put the Winston Cup Series on TV. And thus began the rapidly escalating broadcast contracts with the television networks shoveling additional revenue into NASCAR coffers. But it wasn't until color television, big screens, stereo sound, and cameras mounted in the driver's cockpit looking both to the front and to the rear that the somnambulistic curse of cars driving in circles was made exciting for television viewers.

While expanding the racing audience through television, the actual race schedules each year had gotten out of control with some 50 races to deal with in locations all over the country. It was exhausting for teams and drivers to run their cars two or three times a week in far-flung competitions. The other killers were the short 100-lap or 125-mile races usually run on short tracks. These truncated races used up NASCAR facilities and personnel as much as the longer races but lacked the prestige and the buildup to guarantee big gates and ticket sales. Sponsors also were not happy with investing in the shorter races at smaller tracks due to the return on their advertising dollars. R. J. Reynolds balked at any race shorter than 250 miles for their Winston Cup Series and NASCAR was more than happy to go along.

The 1971 season was the last long season before the schedule was trimmed to 31 races in 1972, the start of the modern era in NASCAR racing.[2]

Just as young Dale Earnhardt was stepping out into his own career following the death of his father, Ralph, in 1972 NASCAR racing was moving rapidly away from those good old days and good old boys who cut their teeth on whiskey tripping in fast cars. Weekend get-togethers at the local cow-pasture track with side money bets kept in a cigar box until after the race had become big corporate business. Once, the local grain and feed store paid $75 to have its name hand-lettered on the door of a 1941 Ford Coupe. By 1972, companies such as STP oil and gas treatment, Valvoline, Quaker State, Delco batteries, and many formerly conservative nonautomotive companies—Kellogg's Corn Flakes, Folgers coffee, McDonald's hamburgers, and Skoal Chewing Tobacco—now sponsored top drivers such as Richard Petty, Bobby Allison, Darrell Waltrip, and David Pearson.

In 1973, the Organization of Petroleum Exporting Countries (OPEC), consisting of mostly Arab and Third World countries, decided to enforce an embargo on petroleum to the United States and European countries. This sudden halt caused a gasoline crisis, which struck at every level of American society. The automobiles built in 1973 were huge with poor gas mileage, and soon long lines began to encircle gas stations so that drivers could get their cars' tanks filled.

The gasoline shortage of 1973–74 affected NASCAR directly at one time in 1974 causing the Daytona 500-mile race to be shortened to 450 miles. Another change of focus impacted the auto industry image. Engine size markings usually painted on the hood or fenders to boast about the powerful mill churning inside were removed. The era of technology-driven competition had been forced aside to emphasize the true stars—the drivers.

As for the cars, a curious transformation took place, a reversal of concept. While Detroit manufacturers scrambled to make cars more gas-efficient, to make them smaller and haul around less iron, they also worked to turn add-ons into standard equipment such as automatic transmission, disc brakes, and early fuel injection. Smaller engines were given four valves per cylinder to improve performance, and air conditioning was made more practical. These innovations trickled down through the showroom cars available to the public through the '70s and '80s. For stock cars racers, however, time would stand still.

Years earlier, the manufacturers used race tracks to experiment with improvements in engines, brakes, exhaust systems, cooling systems, and so forth, and their discoveries found their way to the showroom models, giving the public a kinship with the auto-racing culture. As Detroit said, "Race on Sunday, sell on Monday." But in the 1970s, the homologation employed with the 1969–70 aerocars to force them out of competition was more broadly embraced by NASCAR. Bill France was determined not to let Detroit use NASCAR as a testing bed for their experiments or to create freaks that would never see a public street.

While the original concept for NASCAR was to run pure stock vehicles, that idea was shelved in the 1970s. During the transition period though, the cars still looked like showroom cars with side doors, taped-over and blocked-out headlight apertures, hoods and various sculpted panels and fins; they became anything but stock. The interior cockpit was surrounded with a tubular roll cage, and bench seats were discarded for a single bucket seat. The dashboard was stripped down to basic instrumentation usually minus the speedometer, but with a tachometer that showed engine revolutions. Struts and shocks were heavy duty as were springs, whose stiffness could be altered during the race by adding or reducing wedge. Additional pressure bite could be added to take away from the spring's tension by a mechanic with a socket wrench to improve the car's handling. Turning the wrench counterclockwise twice took two rounds of bite off the spring, or loosened it.

Side doors—before they disappeared altogether—were welded shut and the driver entered and exited through the side window. To ease egress, the steering wheel could be released with a lever. Often, the glass was replaced with sheets of Lexan plastic. To set the car up for each track, various access points to the suspension allowed mechanics to make adjustments in the garage and during the race. Track bars and sway bars kept the car centered over its tires and that centering was checked by examining the tires and tire temperatures across their tread. More or less camber—the angle of the wheel relative to vertical, as viewed from the front or the rear of the car—was adjusted in the suspension to keep the tread correctly placed on the track surface—especially in high-speed turns.

The engines of the 1970s remained for a long time under the homologation rules far behind development of showroom vehicles for the public. While most passenger cars gradually went over to fuel injection, the NASCAR racer continued with a carburetor system dating back 60 years. Street-use cars, besides having the four valves per cylinder also utilized double overhead camshaft engines. Stock cars use cam-in-block engines operating their two valves with push-rods. And the power plants differ wildly. Whereas NASCAR stock engines are limited to 358-cubic inches, the sky's the limit for production cars. Today, even though the cars use names such as Dodge Avenger, Ford Fusion, Chevrolet Impala, and Toyota Camry, which are all front-wheel production cars, the NASCAR versions are all rear-wheel power models.

If the stock cars are so technologically inferior to the passenger cars for sale to the public, how can they haul coal through the banking at 180 miles per hour for 500 miles? The parts in race cars are machined to extremely fine tolerances, fashioned from extremely strong materials, designed to be extremely lightweight while maintaining high tensile strength, and assembled by highly skilled mechanics. An entire team of specialists has only one goal in life—to do everything possible to make that car capable of winning the race. Then the car is given to a very talented driver.

It is interesting that no sooner did NASCAR reverse its policy of running pure stock automobiles than the Sports Car Club of America instituted Showroom Stock car racing in 1972. These cars, with a purchase price ceiling of $3,000 (approximately $14,000 in current currency), are small with 130–152 horsepower motors, stripped of amenities such as air conditioning, sun roofs, and other creature comforts. They have an internal roll cage, six-point safety harness, and a racing seat—with a passenger seat permitted and full race factory suspension. Typical of these cars would be a Dodge Neon. A Competition Race License is required to drive it in competition.

To further cement the eventual goal of across-the-board homologation of the cars, on October 27, 1973, at the Riverside International Raceway in Riverside, California, the green flag fell on the first International Race of Champions (IROC) and a field of identical Porsche Carreras. This first IROC race set the pattern for the following years as the best drivers from NASCAR Winston Cup, NASCAR Busch, World of Outlaws, International Racing League (IRL), dragsters, midgets, you name it, competed in identical cars to see who was the best driver. In 1974, Chevrolet replaced the Carreras with race-prepared Camaros. The series became immensely popular especially after ABC-TV *Wide World of Sports* put a season of IROC racing on its Saturday afternoon program. Special Camaro IROC-Z models appeared—and disappeared from showroom floors

Eventually NASCAR drivers came to dominate the entries and the Camaros were replaced by Dodge Daytonas in 1990. In that 1990 IROC season, the winner was Dale Earnhardt in one of his 11 wins in the series. IROC racing was a good experience for him after all those years chasing points on the Winston Cup Circuit. As race driver Jeff Gordon remembers one practice session:

> The first time I was in IROC we were practicing and I didn't know what I was doing, but he (Earnhardt) certainly did. I got side-by-side with Ken Schrader on the back straight. Dale was behind me and he took me three wide. I decided to look over at Schrader and he was looking straight ahead, real focused and he wasn't going to lift. Then I looked to my left and Dale was just looking over at me grinning. That smile meant he was having so much fun, but he also knew he wasn't going to lift and I was going to lift—and I did.[3]

In 1976, the country's bicentennial year, all of the changes and forces came into play in the Daytona 500 race. On February 15 the sky was clear; the big race that kicked off the NASCAR season had all the big stars buckled into cars that still looked like showroom cars on the outside; and the fans could still spot a Chevy, a Pontiac, a Ford. The fans knew all the numbers of their favorites and the two most recognized were Number 21 of David Pearson and Number 43 of Richard Petty. They had dueled 63 times coming in 1st and 2nd to each other. Here they were again and this time their head-to-head battle—if they survived that long—would be televised live on ABC-TV. The network had negotiated the rights to broadcast the final laps of the contest live.

Before the race, no matter how hard the inspectors tried, their eagle eyes were tested for that edge which some racers felt they needed to be competitive. This time the cheaters got no joy. A. J. Foyt, the Indianapolis 500 three-time champion, was disqualified and knocked off his pole position after a 187.477-mile-per-hour run for having a can of nitrous oxide secreted in his engine compartment. A squirt of that mixture was like jet fuel, enhancing combustion. Another nitrous-oxide user was Darrell Waltrip, and he was bounced along with Dave Marcus, whose mechanic had concealed a blockage in his radiator to raise the temperature and increase the downforce during the race. The three were allowed to requalify but were never a significant threat during the race.

When the green flag dropped, the big, bulky cars rumbled down the white-flag stretch and soared toward the first turn with an unmuffled roar that shook the ground. It was a long race and the sun was setting into the rising cloud of dust and exhaust that hung above Daytona despite the offshore breezes. Petty and Pearson had settled into a duel once again. Petty rolled in for a last splash of gas and tires. In the lowering glare of the setting sun, the pulsing car radiated heat like an open oven. He tore off for the last time, carving a path through slower racers who knew what to do when the red and blue Dodge filled their mirrors. Pearson, running just behind Petty, executed a perfect slingshot pass, using Petty's draft and then suddenly pulling to the side with the gas pedal flat to the floor. He rocketed his red and white Mercury into the lead. The white flag signaling one more lap flashed above them as they rocketed down the main stretch. In the turn, Pearson outgunned Petty's Dodge and retook the lead.

The fans were on their feet. Pit crews stood on their walls. The ABC commentators who had plugged into the race a few laps earlier were hysterical in the booth. Petty and Pearson came down off turn number four flat out boiling toward the finish line. The checkered flag was in the starter's hand, poised to drop. Petty saw Pearson drift slightly off line and drove the Dodge hard down the center of the track as Pearson went high. Trying to shut the door on Pearson, Petty came up toward the outside rail. His right rear fender tipped Pearson's left front fender. At 190 miles per hour the tap slung both cars off line and their spins sent them whirling, swapping ends down the track. Petty kissed the wall and rolled down into the infield. Pearson disappeared into the dust cloud, spinning into the infield.

Petty's Dodge came to rest and he fitfully tried to restart the stalled engine. Pearson had the presence of mind to hammer home the clutch just before impact, so when he was clear of the wall, he let it in and the car restarted while it was still moving.

"Where's Richard? Where's Richard?" Pearson called over his radio as he kept the car rolling. Petty sat helpless as Pearson's front end loomed out of the dust cloud. Streaming water vapor, dragging busted parts and bent metal, Pearson kept his foot on the gas and willed the broken car back up onto the track. At 30 miles per hour, he hissed and rattled across the finish line, the winner. Petty's crew illegally hand-pushed the bent and stalled Dodge until it started and then headed for Pearson's car to beat the stuffing out of him. Richard Petty squeezed out through his driver's side window and stopped his people before any damage could be done. He called to them, "If you have to blame anyone, blame me!"

That finish is considered the most exciting before or since, and after 200 wins and seven championships, Richard Petty still says that's the race everyone will remember—one he lost.

Petty would figure in one more important race that loomed large in NASCAR's expansion and future financial growth, the 1979 Daytona 500. Following the 1976 Daytona shootout and its crowd-pleasing finish all broadcast live on ABC-TV, the networks took a second look. What had been perceived as big cars driving in circles deep in "tall cotton and tabaccy country" suddenly had a nation-wide following. The mid- to late-1970s saw the growth of Citizen's Band radio across the country: passenger-car drivers keyed their CB-radio microphones and joined in with southern truck drivers to gab on the interstate. The South was suddenly "in" with everyone sounding like outtakes from movie blockbuster *Smokey and the Bandit* (1977) or *Convoy* (1978) or even the TV hit of 1979, *The Dukes of Hazzard*, driving fast all over the kudzu-draped boondocks in The General Lee, a highly modified 1969 Dodge Charger. The stock car drivers were smiling, gum chewing, self-effacing good old boys who sounded like truck drivers and airline pilots. But these guys drove hot cars at 190 miles per hour with the possibility of spectacular wrecks around every turn. This state of affairs was pure candy to the TV networks and advertisers. The rural South, which had been laboring under the misleading stereotype of a cheap labor pool living in double-wide trailers on cinder blocks, began to glow with opportunity as a new demographic flocked to stock car races on weekends and bought products that identified with NASCAR cars and drivers.

The 1979 Daytona 500 firmly cemented the television networks' decision to broadcast key races in the NASCAR season. The month of February saw the United States practically shut down from heavy snowfalls in the East and deluge after deluge of rain in the South except in Florida, where the sun shone nicely. TV executives agonized whether the usual blackout of the broadcast (to build attendance at the track) should be lifted in the southern states bordering Florida. As the race drew nearer, the blackout was rescinded and even lifted in Florida as well. Even so, 100,000 spectators showed up and everyone else was trapped in their homes either by snow or rain, and the number of viewers skyrocketed.

The CBS television network had won the rights to broadcast the race flag to flag. For lap after lap, the big sedans blew engines, kissed the wall, and banged into each other. It was a typical race filled with the usual high-speed carnage. And then came the final lap. Bobby Allison and Cale Yarborough had been dueling for the lead with A. J. Foyt, Richard Petty, and Darrell Waltrip, back in the pack battling for 3rd. The crowd came to its feet as the two leaders swapped paint running high, low, anywhere they could find running room for the dash to the checkered flag. Allison saw a chance to shove Yarborough down low onto the track apron. The cars banged together, and finally both cars lost it and sailed into the wall, caroming off and streaming smoke and sparks down into the grass. The CBS broadcasters babbled with excitement as the cameras peered into the dust and debris-filled field to pick out the new leader.

Howling out of the dust cloud came red and blue Dodge Number 43 with Richard Petty at the wheel grinning at the prize he had been handed. Waltrip dogged him right to the finish line, but Petty, who had not won a race in 18 months, roared beneath the checkered flag line, and the grandstands exploded with cheers. The King had done it again. Meanwhile, in the infield, Yarborough's and Allison's cars had bumped to a steaming stop and the drivers tumbled out onto the grass. Shouts were exchanged. Bobby's brother Donnie parked his car and joined the fray. Soon everyone was flailing at each other with fists and feet until crewmen and officials separated the combatants. Merciless TV cameras missed none of it.

At about the time Dale Earnhardt was beginning his successful quest for the NASCAR Rookie of the Year, NASCAR was setting itself up for exponential growth in the 1980s. Old dirt tracks were being razed and the land turned into condominium developments, and new amenity-laden paved ovals were rising in their place. Short tracks were refurbished and superspeedways were laying down their high-banked turns and media booths for press and television cameras.

Drivers were trying to figure out how to spend all the money they were making while car owners studied the cost of corporate jet planes that could land on short runways near racetrack towns. A new prosperity from sponsorships and larger purses had the upper echelon of drivers and owners living large. Some of that largesse trickled down to the racers who were just beginning to make their marks, but it was still a hard life to race for a living.

## NOTES

1. Joe Menzer, *The Wildest Ride: A History of NASCAR* (New York: Simon & Schuster, 2001), p. 183.

2. Mike Hembree, *NASCAR: The Definitive History of America's Sport* (New York: Harper Entertainment, 2000), pp. 126–129.

3. The Earnhardt Connection, "Earnhardt in IROC," http://www.dale earnhardt.net/iroc/.

# Chapter 12

# GROWING UP AT LAST

Sizing up Dale Earnhardt as a life partner must have been a daunting task for Teresa Houston. She first met Dale in 1974, introduced to him by her father, car driver Hal Houston, at the Hickory Motor Speedway owned by her uncle Tommy Houston. She was 16 and Dale was 23. Teresa was part of the stock car racing–culture and a pretty girl with chestnut brown hair and eyes set off by high cheekbones and a wide mouth. By the mid-1970s, Dale had developed into a tall, rangy guy with a signature mustache and a triangular face that smiled easily with deep blue eyes flanked by deep creases. The advantage Teresa had growing up around fast cars, the men who drove them, and those who owned them was a knowledge of the business that came by way of osmosis, swigging down an ice cold, dripping wet Coca-Cola while mechanics and a driver turned the air blue with cusses as they tried to reseat some transmission gears; or hearing the phone calls that shaped deals; or getting her best shoes filthy stepping into oil sludge on the garage floor. A pretty girl in the pits and garage was a challenge to the young guys who saw that same energy and spark. Some of the older veterans treated her like a daughter or with elaborate southern courtesy. That was all part of being a member of a race car extended family. She was also very smart, blowing through high school in three years and then taking courses in interior design at the local community college.

Dale and Teresa didn't begin dating until 1978 when she was 20 and he was 27. He came with two children and a third being raised by his stepfather because he couldn't pay the child-support payments. He also came with a career that was the most important thing in his life. She was second as were Dale's two previous wives, who could not play second fiddle to a dirt-track race car. She could live in a little third-rate house outside Charlotte while he raced for small dirt-track purses like his daddy had done until he was an old man still in his 40s. But she insisted on controlling what happened after the flag fell each weekend. She took on managing his career.

She helped him with his finances, what he wore, what he ate, and when he started to gather a fan base, what his hats and T-shirts should look like and their price. Two years after they started dating, she and Dale formed Dale Earnhardt Inc., which would grow to become a multimillion-dollar empire.

By 1982, NASCAR's image as a rowdy collection of former whiskey trippers and backwoods good old boys had been wiped away. NASCAR was now a family, as were the sponsors who used the drivers to sell their products. A strong suggestion was made to Dale and Teresa—who were living together—that they get married. It was an easy next step for them both.[1] For the rest of his life, she was at his side figuratively and literally so he could focus on driving and winning. In the 1980s, that focus would be strongly tested.

No sooner had Earnhardt won NASCAR Rookie of the Year in 1979 with the Rod Osterlund team that speculation began concerning future wins. Dale's crew chief Jake Elder, who prepared the Monte Carlo, told the press, "I really believe this is only the start. I think you will see the boy win some more short track races and I'm even looking at a couple of super speedway wins. He's young and he's good. If he don't get hurt, he's got at least 12 good years ahead."[2]

Ten months passed before Earnhardt's next NASCAR test, this time at Daytona during Speed Week before the big 500-mile race. On February 10, 1980, he piloted the Osterlund Oldsmobile 20 laps—50 miles—in the brief Busch Clash for a $50,000 paycheck. He reached the checkered flag ahead of Neil Bonnett, Darrell Waltrip, Cale Yarborough, and Richard Petty toward the back of the pack. Having tested his abilities on the Daytona International Speedway over a short haul, the next step up was the Atlanta 500 run at the Atlanta International Raceway in Hampton, Georgia, on March 15. There, he ran the Osterlund Monte Carlo from a 31st spot on the starting grid to 1st place. Though he won his first 500-mile superspeedway, he had engine problems at the outset resulting in the poor starting position. The 2nd-place car driven by Rusty Wallace also experienced engine trouble and finished nine seconds behind Earnhardt. His only real challenge was Donnie Allison, Bobby's brother, who was slowed by engine misfires around lap 300. Keeping the lead, Earnhardt could only hope his engine would hold out until the end because it was running at 270 degrees.

The 500-mile races carried more prestige than the shorter runs, so the team of Earnhardt and Osterlund returned to Bristol for the Valleydale Southeastern 500 on March 30. A 500-mile race on a short half-mile track is a lot of work because of the short straights and the constant turns. Earnhardt's average speed was 97 miles per hour, but his key to victory was the Osterlund pit crew, which got him out of the pits after gas fill-up and tire changes under the green light ahead of Darrell Waltrip for the lead on lap 366.

After he rolled the Chevy into victory lane, Earnhardt told reporters, "I really thought it would take a year to win my first race."[3]

As the team unloaded at the Nashville Raceway in Tennessee for the Busch Nashville 420, other drivers and crews waited patiently for the Sophomore Jinx to catch up with Earnhardt. Other second-year drivers had stumbled after their first year of flashy success. The kid from Kannapolis seemed to be a different breed of cat. He took risks, drove aggressively—too aggressively some said—and drove the wheels off the Osterlund Chevy without mercy. This time, Cale Yarborough pressed Earnhardt hard, but failed to rattle the myth-buster who crossed the finish line out in front by four car lengths in front of 16,799 standing cheering fans. Veterans Petty and Waltrip were noncontenders with Petty's car failing to get up to speed in the straights while Waltrip suffered through a long pit stop on lap 291.

Earnhardt added $14,600 to his winnings for his third Winston Cup win in 54 starts. "Not too many people knew any of us two years ago," he said. "But our team has it together. I'm proud of my team and I can't say enough good things about them boys."[4]

The Martinsville Speedway is a short tough track with single file turns, and the Old Dominion 500 race run on September 28 wrung every drop of capability out of the Osterlund Chevy. Short tracks are also hard on brakes due to the constant turning around the oval. That fact was brought home to the Osterlund team when Earnhardt came zooming in for his pit stop with virtually zero brakes left and overshot the box. After hand-heaving the big hot Chevy back to its correct spot in the paint, the crew watched other cars rush past back out onto the track. Martinsville exacted its usual toll and only 14 cars were left running at the end of the day out of 31 that took the green flag.

Fall leaves were scurrying down the sidewalks in Kannapolis, North Carolina, as friends and neighbors of the Earnhardts' piled kids and coolers into cars and pick-up trucks for a run to the Charlotte Motor Speedway in Harrisburg, North Carolina. Dale, the hometown kid who had been winning Grand National races, was set to run in the National 500.

With this run, he could clinch the 1980 Grand National Championship after winning the 1979 Rookie of the Year.

With 4,217 points working for him—115 points ahead of Cale Yarborough—this win could do the job. And that is how it worked out, as he beat Yarborough to the finish line by 1.83 seconds. That win totaled up his winnings for the season to $432,675. And the hometown crowd returned to Kannapolis to celebrate their new champion.

That Winston Cup win was the only one Rod Osterlund would celebrate as a car owner. As the team headed into the 1981 season, Osterlund, a land developer, began experiencing financial shortfalls and the cost of the team became a drag. In the middle of that season, without warning, Osterlund sold the team to J. D. Stacy who did not meet Earnhardt's standards as a car owner. After four desultory races, he quit the Stacy team.

That year was a big year for controversy among the drivers and NASCAR. The ever-changing rules for competitive cars handed down by NASCAR shifted away from the big sedans to downsized cars with 110-inch wheel bases. It had taken Detroit time to counter the gas guzzlers of the mid- to late-'70s and come up with compact designs. Now they were mandated for use on the world's fastest racetrack for the start of the 1981 season.

When the Daytona International Speedway track opened, drivers were venturing into the unknown for the first and the fastest race on a long track. The aerodynamics, chassis setups, tires, spoiler effects, drafting capabilities in a pack of cars—all were question marks until test time a few days before the big race. Almost as soon as the smaller cars were rolled out, complaints streamed into the pits. The downsized cars were loose—they lacked the stability of the bigger vehicles. In a high-speed draft, this floating sensation took away the feel of the wheels on the track. At 200 miles per hour—and the cars were capable of that speed—this instability gave the drivers nervous jitters. For turn after turn, they would not only have to race but keep their car under some kind of marginal control to avoid contact.

Richard Petty, whose Petty Enterprises had been loyal to Chrysler products, was now faced with a decision. Richard had a Dodge Mirada rolled out during the tests, and 15,000 spectators—and Chrysler fans—turned up at the track to watch this critical run. Petty horsed the small Dodge around the track, trying to find some degree of finesse in its handling. The speed was also eight miles per hour slower than the other cars. He had no luck and for the race, reverted to a somewhat heavier Buick. It was in that car that he drove to victory at the 1981 Daytona 500.

The compact cars were fitted with large spoilers that added traction gripping downforce on their rear decks, which helped with their twitchy feel. The homologation also made it difficult to break away from the pack since all the cars were evenly powered and set up and 49 lead changes were recorded. During the 31-race season, 772 lead changes occurred—a record that was never broken.

As for Earnhardt, he did not win a race all year, but he did make one connection that would eventually change his life and career direction. In August 1981, Earnhardt signed on with car owner Richard Childress.[5]

A former driver who began as an independent back in 1971, Childress never won a race. He got his first major NASCAR ride back when Bill France bucked the union organizers before the Talladega Superspeedway race, and 32 drivers packed up and left the garages in protest. Childress was one of the replacement drivers recruited to fill in the field. He developed as a journeyman driver, never winning a race, but staying near the front enough times to register 6 top-5 and 76 top-10 finishes. In 1976, he managed a 3rd place for his career best.

Childress decided to retire as a driver in 1981 and tend to his other businesses. He would go on to become one of the richest men in North Carolina. About that time, Dale Earnhardt was looking for a ride and R. J. Reynolds, sponsor of the Winston Cup Grand National Series, suggested to Childress that Earnhardt might be a good anchor around which to build a race team. Personally, he and Dale became friends and Earnhardt signed on for the year.

While their partnership flourished on a personal level, professionally, nothing seemed to work, and Childress was aware that his crew and car combination was not up to Earnhardt's driving capabilities. He suggested Dale find another ride with a winning organization until the Childress team could be improved. Reluctantly, but seeing the wisdom in the move, Earnhardt left the Childress organization and signed on with Bud Moore Engineering for the 1982 season.

Earnhardt did not come in empty-handed. He had been approached by Wrangler Jeans, which was looking for a suitable manly image for its denim pants, a sports figure who could easily live up to its motto "One Tough Customer." Earnhardt's take-no-prisoners driving style, his rugged good looks at age 30, and natural affinity for western wear fit the image perfectly.

By 1982, Dale Earnhardt's life was settling in. He had divorced Brenda Gee and now had custody of his three children and that same year, he married Teresa Houston and everyone was moved into his home on Lake Norman just outside of Charlotte.

Walter M. "Bud" Moore from Spartanburg, South Carolina, was a veteran car owner who returned home from World War II and started his racing career as crew chief for Buck Baker in 1957. He had a good reputation for getting the most out of his cars and put quite a few trophies on the shelf proving it. At one time or another, most of the greats of American stock car racing drove for him including: Fireball Roberts, David Pearson, Cale Yarborough, Bobby Isaac, Darrell Waltrip, Donnie Allison, Geoff Bodine, Ricky Rudd, Brett Bodine, and Morgan Shepherd.

Dale Earnhardt climbed into a Bud Moore–prepared Ford Thunderbird on April 4, 1982, at the Darlington International Raceway and rolled into his first victory after the year-long drought. For the CMC Chemicals Rebel 500, the Moore team proved to be particularly canny when they removed the tires he had used to qualify the car and set them aside. Much later in the race, they put them back on when it counted for those final laps. That maneuver and one round of bite taken out of the suspension set the car up to run all day at an average of 127.544 miles per hour. It was a race where sheer power counted as Cale Yarborough, the only serious challenger, rode his bumper right in behind Earnhardt on the final lap looking to make a slingshot pass on the inside flying out of Earnhardt's draft. As the two cars powered out of turn number three, the flat-out throttle of the Bud Moore Thunderbird gave Dale a half-car length win at the finish line.

That was Earnhardt's only win for the 1982 season. He finished 12th in the points ratings. In 1983, he managed to push the Bud Moore T-Birds up to 8th place with wins at the Daytona 125-mile Qualifier, the Busch 420 at Nashville, and the Talladega 500. While he failed again to win the big prize, the Daytona 500, he won the Talladega Superspeedway in front of 100,000 race fans and the lenses of CBS-TV. He dodged one bullet when Neil Bonnett was put out of the race on the first lap after his engine exploded.

"My engine blew going into the third turn. It just exploded, driving the crankshaft through the engine. My oil got all over the place and that's when everybody started spinning in the fourth turn."[6]

As Earnhardt was trying to find his way back into victory lane aboard Moore's Thunderbirds in 1982 and 1983, three phenomena were brewing in stock car racing. First, as Earnhardt's responsibilities increased at home with his new wife, three kids, and the growing side businesses created by his investments, the need to win or at least finish high in points became critical. Toward that end, his driving style—already considered a throwback to the dirt- track days—became even more aggressive. As Humpy Wheeler noted, "People don't like to see [Earnhardt's] car on their bumper. They just don't. Now Richard Petty, he was okay on your back bumper. David Pearson, he was okay. But you didn't want to see [Earnhardt's] car."[7]

The second phenomenon was Earnhardt's sudden rise in popularity—if you could call it that. Through the 1980s, his driving style and the way he carried himself off the track—all loose and cowboy-like—ready with a joke and no excuses if the race took a bad turn, caught on with the public. Women found him handsome and sexy. Men admired his over-the-top attitude and how he backed up his lifestyle with his driving skills. And there were also those fans who booed him on the track (but never to his face—that seemed a bit too dangerous) and threw chicken bones and debris at his car as it rolled past, which was a danger to all the racers. However deep this dislike ran though, it only brought the detractors to the track to see what nasty bit of driving he'd try to pull off this week.

Finally, there was "Jaws." Darrell Waltrip, a major NASCAR competitor had the gift of gab. He would not shut up. In the garage, in the pits, in the car, in front of a microphone, he was by far the most gregarious of the drivers. He was also a good driver and, because of that skill, often found himself seeing Earnhardt's car slide in behind him fairly oozing with malicious intent. Time after time Waltrip and Earnhardt found themselves entangled. Waltrip carried on his war of words off the track, suggesting one time that drivers should be awarded 10 extra points in a race for spinning Earnhardt off the track.

The taciturn Earnhardt, often at a loss for a verbal comeback, had no problem making his presence felt howling around a track slick with rubber, slipping and sliding around the competition, tucking his front bumper in where it would do him the most good.

At one race, Waltrip was driving a Junior Johnson car and closing in on Earnhardt, who was leading. Waltrip called on his radio, "I'm gonna make my move on the backstretch!" Johnson in the pits bit his lip. He wanted Waltrip to make his pass on a turn. He knew Earnhardt's bad habits. "All right," Johnson called back, "but don't you clear him! Because the second you think you've cleared him, he'll turn you!"

Waltrip blasted past Earnhardt on the backstretch, but as they flew into turn three, Earnhardt hooked his front bumper into Waltrips's right rear quarter panel and that bump caused the Chevrolet to turn and careen hard into the outside guardrail and bounce down into the infield. The action also caused Earnhardt's car to fishtail and spin out into the grass. Both cars were out of the race as well as those of Geoff Bodine and Joe Ruttman, who had been making their own run on the leaders.

An angry Junior Johnson shouted later, "You can't race with a fool like that!"

Of course Junior's blowup seemed like the pot calling the kettle black since he had driven with the same ruthless abandon during his driving days in the 1960s. Earnhardt only offered his lopsided grin and commented, "Helluva show, wasn't it?"

Their rivalry helped fill seats around the tracks where they raced. Jaws continued his never-ending barrage of put-downs to anyone who would listen. In later years, when Waltrip needed a ride to rekindle his driving fortunes, it was Dale Earnhardt who gave him a car and let him finish his driving career in style.

At the end of the 1983 season, Richard Childress returned as he said he would, this time with a formidable team, and asked Dale to drive for him in the 1984 season. Childress had not been idle. He had sewn up a deal with General Motors for parts so he could build Chevy race cars from scratch, controlling every part that went into the vehicle. He had also made a deal with Goodyear for tires and was ready to field a crew that was drilled to perfection. Dale took up residence in the Childress shop once again, bringing his Wrangler sponsorship with him and the two high school dropouts began dreaming of a racing empire.

The Talladega 500 that ran on July 29, 1984, proved to be yet another face-off between Earnhardt and Waltrip circling the 2.66-mile track. This time, however, Earnhardt was well mounted aboard the Childress Chevrolet Monte Carlo and desperate for a win after a dry spell of 30 winless races.

When the white flag fell, signifying one more lap to run, it was Terry Labonte in the lead driving a Chevy, with Earnhardt and Buddy Baker in a Ford chasing him down. Coming into the last lap, Earnhardt drafted Labonte's Chevy very closely and then pulled a slingshot pass—but instead of diving down to the inside, Earnhardt let centrifugal force work with the draft and passed Labonte high on the outside. Drafting behind him was Baker, raising the speed of both cars. When Earnhardt dropped down he was in the lead with Baker inching up. Yet again, the fans were on their feet as the two cars screamed hub-to-hub out of the final turn and barreled toward the finish line. Drawing ahead, inch by inch, the Childress Chevy arrived at the line 1.66 seconds ahead of Baker. It took a photo to determine the winner.

At age 33, Earnhardt was back on the winner's podium with Teresa at his side. He was also $47,100 richer.

His next win at the Atlanta International Raceway proved his ability to bring a sick car home and the durability of the Childress entry. In the lead with only 19 laps to go, a piece of the Chevy's header pipe broke off during the 500-mile race and punctured a small hole in the oil pan. Immediately, the car began throwing oil, some of which ended up on Geoff Bodine's windshield, forcing the challenger to back off. Seeing smoke and sparks, Earnhardt instinctively backed off the gas as well and nursed the car along until he decided it would hold together for enough laps to win. Then his alternator blew, cutting off electricity to his spark plugs except from his battery supply. Knowing his car, he held his pace, estimating there was enough power left in the battery to finish. Behind him, Bill Elliott was flat out on the gas, closing fast. With everything pushed to the firewall, Earnhardt could only steer and watch Elliott's hood creep up alongside, its engine roar blending with the blast from his own crippled mill. Earnhardt's front bumper crossed the finish line 0.57 seconds ahead of Elliott. The audience collapsed back into their seats. Their guy had done it again.

## NOTES

1. Marshall Brooks, interview with the author, Concord, NC, October 16, 2008.

2. Steve Waid, "Earnhardt Wins Southeastern 500," in *The Earnhardt Collection: Because Winning Matters* (Chicago, IL: Triumph Books and Charlotte, NC: Street & Smith's Sports Publications, 2006), p. 11.

3. Ibid., pp. 16–17.

4. Gene Granger, "Yarborough Fails to Rattle Sophomore," in *The Earnhardt Collection: Because Winning Matters*, pp. 18–19.

5. Famous Sports Stars, "Dale Earnhardt Sr.—Guts Make a Champ," http://sports.jrank.org/pages/1298/Earnhardt-Dale-Sr-Guts-Make-Champ.html.

6. Waid, p. 31

7. Joe Menzer, *The Wildest Ride: A History of NASCAR* (New York: Simon & Schuster, 2001), p. 247.

# Chapter 13

# THE BIG BUSINESS OF NASCAR—1980s AND BEYOND

It is the fast and furious action that keeps fans filing through the turnstiles and driving their RVs to set up housekeeping at their nearest—and often distant—tracks. NASCAR has grown into a swirling bottomless pit of cash and rewards administered by a virtual army of employees across the nation. From the mid-1980s to the present, the shift from a technological auto-mobile-centric sport to driver worship opened the door to a river of cash sponsorships, both for the drivers and crews and the races themselves.

Mark Martin dissected Jeff Gordon's win at the 1998 Brickyard 400 race at the Indianapolis Speedway, which offered the largest purse up to that time, a total of $1,600,000 for about three hours work. It breaks down as follows:

| | |
|---|---|
| Race purse and TV money | $270,875 |
| NASCAR Car Owners Winners Circle Award | $10,200 |
| NASCAR Plan 1 Award | $7,000 |
| Winston Leader Bonus (winner and points leader) | $10,000 |
| Third-Place Qualifying Award | $2,500 |
| Defending Winston Cup Series Champion Award | $5,000 |
| PPG Winner's Trophy Award (from rack) | $225,000 |

Martin, one of today's top veteran drivers, compares this kind of pay-day to Gordon's winnings from 1993 to 2003. He won 64 races and four NASCAR Cup Championships for a total of $58,525,057. Even drivers who only complete two-thirds of a couple of seasons' races and have no wins or top-10 finishes can bring home over $400,000 for each season.[1]

The downside is having to call it quits by the time you reach your late 40s, which gives you about 20 years to build your nest egg and then seek new employment. Unlike championship golf where players can compete into their 60s, race car driving requires such a high level of physical and judgment skills that the body requires more time to adjust after each race. There is also the stress of having a bad year when your lifestyle has caught up to your good year income. And then there is the possibility of being crippled or killed. Toward reducing that unfortunate end, NASCAR has committed millions of dollars in research and development to create a safer car.

Close finishes build large grosses at the ticket booth, which was the reason for holding so close to the homologation rules. But sameness made for dull racing if no one could pass or break away from the pack. Crew chiefs had to fall back upon their shade tree mechanic days and looked for ways to boost performance within the restrictive rules. A. J. Foyt got caught with a can of nitrous oxide tubed into his fuel line. When released, it gave the engine a power boost. He had to requalify without it. Air cowls appeared that drew air rushing over the surface of the car and directed it into the carburetor not unlike a supercharger. Dale Earnhardt became an outspoken champion for shutting those vents off. NASCAR chose to permit them on some races, but not on others.

Car sales became less tied to success of the Detroit brand of car that won on Sunday and the manufacturers were feeling the pinch of imports, so designing and building limited-run racing cars such as the aerocars of 1969–70 became prohibitive. It was the vast resources of corporate NAS-CAR that finally settled the impasse to—almost—everyone's satisfaction.

With engine size, fuel capacity, tires, and the ability to level the horse-power separation between cars under control, aerodynamics became the critical variable. To the already massive pre- and postrace car inspection requirements was added wind tunneling to determine inequality of body streamlining. Each car was rolled into the tunnel and a huge fan blew across the bodywork, and its speed over various parts of the body was measured to determine drag on the car as though it was moving. Each wind-tunneling inspection cost the car owner $16,000. Childress/Earn-hardt drove into the 1986 season sporting a sharply slanted rear window and a reduced spoiler angle on their Chevy Monte Carlo.

Aerodynamics of the side panels, rear deck, wheel wells, and sloping hood down to the once squared-off front end came under scrutiny. As research moved forward while season after season played out in front of the crowds, a set of 22 templates was created from machined aluminum.

These templates were laid on the bodywork to see how the slope and angle of each panel fit the predetermined shape decided on by NASCAR as optimum. The largest of these—called The Claw—laid across the entire hood and roofline.

Drivers who continued to test these ideas in competition and on empty tracks found little cheer in the new generation of racers coming out of NASCAR. On the other hand, Humpy Wheeler who had worked up from tire manufacturer's rep and now owned the racetracks at Bristol, Atlanta, Charlotte, and others in the west had the last word: "Right now we're fighting constantly to keep cars competitive and it's difficult to do with different body styles. You can do all the wind-tunnel testing you want, but until you get on a track, and until you get the cars in a drafting situation, you really don't know." Wheeler continued, "I know the purists will scream, but we are in the entertainment business first and, without that, nothing else exists. We'd rather have the fans discussing the drivers' performances at the races—not the mechanical rules. We're not that far from a common body today."[2]

NASCAR's idea was to make the main body templates the same for all makes of cars with approved front end and tail sections for each brand. It was left for the team to use paint and decals to indicate headlamps, taillamps, grill, and brand identification to tell a Chevy from a Dodge from a Ford, Pontiac, or whatever was running that season. This would make the Winston Cup similar to the International Race of Champions for the 1970s. Already, the stock cars of the modern era carry the names of front-engine, front-drive cars, but run with iron V-8s and rear-wheel drive for simplicity. Over the '80s and '90s the hood lines were lowered, front ends became more rounded, and fenders hugged the tires as the body hunkered down toward the track level. From a souped up friendly family sedan, the NASCAR ideal vehicle had become almost malevolent, a feral thing that crouched in the pit box, its engine turning over with a guttural idle, challenging the driver to turn it loose.

Al Pearce, in an interview with car owner Jack Roush for *Popular Mechanics* magazine quoted Roush when he said, "I have been a proponent of common templates for a long time. I'm not talking about enough templates to egg-crate the car. I think we have twice as many templates as we need. I think that of the 22 templates, four or five could be common, with each template built to the shortest applicable dimension among the competing cars. Then you'd need unique templates for each manufacturer in the areas of bumpers, headlights, taillights and those things that define the uniqueness of the car. We could have a common roof, a common hood, a common decklid, a common windshield, a common side panel, and a common rear spoiler dimension and shape, with different treatments for the front and rear fascias, and there's still plenty of differentiation there for the manufacturers."[3]

Kevin Trilett, director of operations for NASCAR, added, "We spent six to eight months on the common templates project starting in 1998, then put it on the back burner. We've been going to the wind tunnel periodically . . . impounding cars after a race for the tests, because aero was becoming more important than horsepower. We used the wind tunnel as an educational tool. We've gone back to the tunnel more and more frequently, but a large percentage of our decisions are still based on on-track performance, start to finish. We're looking at the whole spectrum, from doing nothing more, to allowing minor modifications, to making all the cars very similar. We haven't ruled anything out, including the option of a single body shell."

That single body shell seems to be where American stock car racing is headed. Taking a quick time-machine jump into the future that awaited the drivers of the mid-1980s, the new cars evolved in a predictable direction that anyone who took the time back in 1986 could have seen coming. On January 11, 2006, NASCAR announced the Car of Tomorrow (CoT for short) that would pave the way for the all-purpose race car. The design program was begun in 1998 to create this ideal body shape and power plant combination culminating aerodynamic tests and cost estimates that supposedly will level out the playing field for small shops and large multiteam operations. Everybody gets a fair bite at the apple.

The evolution of the CoT has not come about without a lot of compromises and negotiations. Some drivers love the idea while others hate it. The Big Three auto manufacturers are withholding full approval until they see whether they can continue to support race cars that have little or nothing to do with what they sell their customers. Since the battle between drivers and NASCAR at Talladega when it opened for its 500-mile race, NASCAR's sanguine position on presenting spectacle and speed without concern for tires shredding has reversed, and the CoT represents safety at the cost of individuality.

While the overall first impression of this new concept has become menacing, it is also rounded at the corners like a bumper car at the county fair. The raw energy projected by the sedan-like angles and thrusting fenders of the 1980s transition cars is lost. What made the car-chase scene in *Bullitt* starring Steve McQueen so exciting was seeing big-shouldered Detroit iron slammed around the streets and hills of San Francisco. That was Hollywood with stunt men and carefully choreographed action, but it was visceral. People in the audience had cars like those in the theater parking lot or at home in the garage.

Evolution in design had always been a follow-the-leader process as with the Childress/Earnhardt Chevy of 1986 with its deeply slanted rear window displacing the chopped-off back-window silhouette of the standard Monte Carlo. The cars of 1998, when the program began, were almost all based on a design by Holman-Moody, first used for the 1966 Ford Fairlane. The primary design considerations at that time were safety innovations, performance and competition, and cost efficiency for teams.[4]

The CoT car mandated in 2006 for the 2007 season is two inches taller and four inches wider. The driver's seat has been moved four inches to the right and the roll cage shifted three inches to the rear. All around the driver, crumple zones have been created in case of collision. Up front, the air dam has been replaced by a splitter that increases the downforce on the front of the car to hold it to the track surface at high speed. Engine exhaust is no longer piped through the cockpit and out the rear but is vented out the right front side keeping the heat away from the driver. Fuel is stored in a stronger cell that is also smaller, holding 17¾ gallons instead of the previous 22. This reduction guarantees more pit stops and chances for lead changes during the race.

## NOTES

1. Mark Martin, NASCAR for Dummies, 2nd Edition (Hoboken, NJ: Wiley, 2003), pp. 162–163.

2. Al Pearce, "Midseason NASCR Update: The Agony of Victory," Popular Mechanics, http://www.popularmechanics.com/automotive/motorsports/1268721.html?page=5.

3. Ibid.

4. Brian Watkins, "Car of Tomorrow—A Bridge Too Far," http://www.insider racingnews.com.

# Chapter 14

# FORTUNES TURN AROUND

Dale Earnhardt saddled up his Wrangler Monte Carlo for two wins in 1984, first at Talladega and then at the Atlanta Journal 500, where Bill Elliott of Dawsonville, Georgia, was the favorite for the rain-delayed event. But with only 25 laps remaining, Elliott's engine began to douse the track with oil, which splattered across his windshield and made hard racing impossible. Earnhardt kept on, steady over the oil-slicked asphalt as he had learned to handle soaked dirt on hinterland mud tracks in his rapidly disappearing youth.

It was on lap 129 that the novice racer Terry Schoonover lost his car on a turn, smacked the wall hard, and smoked down into the infield. As the other cars streaked around the grass embankment where Schoonover had come to rest, emergency crews carved away the car's rook until they could get at the driver. He was dead in the car and they took his body away in an EMS truck. Deaths at the wheel were no longer as common as the old days when fire or rollovers burned and crushed drivers, smashing cheap helmets like eggshells and sending up cotton T-shirts or grease-stained overalls into incendiary death traps. There were broken bones and bruises, but the game was getting safer every year.

The short tracks were kind to Earnhardt in 1985. At Richmond Fairgrounds Raceway on February 24, he won the battle of the pit stops managing to barely miss getting wiped out by his pal Neil Bonnett driving for Junior Johnson. Of the 30 cars that started down the scarred track, only 16 stayed on their wheels to take the checkered flag.

At the half-mile Bristol track, he took the Valleydale 500 on April 6, another bruising race that set a record 15 caution flags over the

3-hour-and-15-minute race. This time, Earnhardt was chasing Ricky Rudd aboard a fast Thunderbird. Around they went with Earnhardt losing Rudd in the straights every time. Then, on lap 477, a final caution flag was thrown and both Rudd and Earnhardt pitted. Earlier, Earnhardt had blistered his left front tire and it had slowed him. Now he got fresh rubber on the left side while Rudd took on right-side rubber. Both cars blew back out onto the track for the charge to the finish line. The new tires made the difference and while Earnhardt's handling improved, Rudd's fell apart as the new tires caused the car to push to the right. The best Rudd could do was hold his 2nd place and watch Earnhardt power under the checkered flag ahead of him for the win.

At both Bristol on August 24 and at Martinsville on September 22, the physical side of stock car racing had the tracks littered with debris and spinning cars. Once again, Earnhardt demonstrated his skill in the short track bull rings. He traded bumps and swapped paint with the other drivers and, curiously, was nowhere to be seen when the worst crack-ups scattered Detroit metal all over the track.

Tim Richmond groused after the races about Earnhardt's "pulling the same stunt" wacking fenders when it suited him and then getting upset when the favor was returned. Earnhardt managed to win four races in 1985 with Richard Childress–prepared Chevrolets, but it was 1986 that changed everything and set up the team for the next 10 years.

Bill Elliott's Bud Moore–prepared Ford Thunderbird was proving to be the hot ticket car. In 1985, the T-Bird's sloped and rounded design beat up the field with 11 superspeedway wins and proved to be virtually undraftable. Elliott just missed the 1985 championship by a series of problems late in the season running the short tracks—one of those problems being Earnhardt.

As with the aerocars of 1969–70, an aerowar broke out in 1986 that sucked in all the manufacturers and drivers, searching for the slickest combination of reduced wind resistance and increased wind assistance to get an edge on speed. To counter the Thunderbird threat and aware that lights were on and welding torches flickered in other garages as well, Chevrolet, in partnership with Cars and Concepts (C&C) developed an aerodynamically improved Monte Carlo. C&C essentially built the car with General Motors looking on using race-oriented parts and testing each element in a wind tunnel at the GM Proving Grounds. The Monte Carlo had been introduced as a somewhat boxy passenger sedan back in 1970 and both downsized and reshaped until this latest version. Two hundred white and burgundy Monte Carlo Aero Coupes (or "SS" for Super Sport in the street version) were run off the line to comply with NASCAR's production rule that a sufficient number of the cars must be available to the public. Of the 200, 35 had custom plastic sloped rear windows, which were sent to the NASCAR teams for developmental study. The remaining 165 cars were shipped, one at a time, to southeastern dealers in South Carolina, Florida, North Carolina, Alabama, and Georgia, where they were scooped up at premium prices.

Slope-backed cars were introduced by Buick and Oldsmobile at the same time as the Chevy's rear plastic-glass sloped greenhouse bolted to the rear deck rolled out. To keep up with the slick look, Pontiac, the weak sister of the group, pushed a nasty-looking Grand Prix 2+2 with a flush grill and rear-glass area that looked as big as a swimming pool atrium. Computer-aided design (CAD) had definitely arrived in garage row.

One of the casualties of these new sloped and rounded designs coming from the manufacturers and their consulting partners was the ability to draft. Passing on high-speed tracks demanded the draft, which used wind passing over the aerodynamic shape of the lead car to literally suck the following car tucked in directly behind the leader into a partnership that increased the speed of both by removing the air turbulence immediately behind the leader car, which had an unwanted braking effect. The combination of sloping hood, roof, and rear-deck lines culminating in a downforce inducing spoiler left little air to suck along the following car. At high speed—200 miles per hour and up—what had been a literal train of cars rushing through the turns and down the straights reverted to a loose collection of individual cars unable to get around the car in front due to the similarities of power plant, tires, and so forth. More and more the races were relying on caution flags for position changes. Pit stops, blown engines, and cut tires were deciding many races' outcomes rather than skilled driving.

Dale Earnhardt did not care. He was his daddy's son and felt just as comfortable in a slick car on a speed-slippery track as he had in the loosey-goosey dirt cars where he learned his craft slip-sliding in the mud. Now, he aimed his new fast Chevy like a bullet at the 1986 season.

# Chapter 15

# THE INTIMIDATOR TAKES COMMAND

The gloves came off in 1986 beginning with the Busch Clash, that 20-lap, 50-mile sprint around the two-mile Daytona tri-oval. Driving the Childress Wrangler Chevrolet Monte Carlo SS, Earnhardt grabbed the lead from his pal Neil Bonnett on the sixth lap and went on to win. He was challenged hard by the hot dog of 1985, Bill Elliott, driving a Ford Thunderbird. Elliott pressed Earnhardt on the long fast straights, but the new Chevrolet SS sliced faster through the curves. Riding high into each curve and drifting down as he came out, Earnhardt left Elliott no draft to follow—especially with the Chevy's new aerodynamic shape.

All pretenses had stopped with the Detroit car builders to offer up stock-appearing bodies for race modification. Chevrolet led the way in 1986 with the Monte Carlo SS Aero Coupe. The Monte Carlo had been introduced as a somewhat boxy passenger sedan back in 1970 and both downsized and reshaped until this latest version. The rear half of the body shell received a makeover as the rear window was slanted back in a semi-fast-back configuration and the spoiler was flattened out, becoming less of an air dam and more of a directional device. This Super Sport body style was stamped out in a series of 200. This number was not arbitrary but matched the latest requirements of the NASCAR rules for a stock body. Back in 1969–70, the era of the aerocars that had swept up the prizes, the car makers had been required to produce at least 1,200 of any new design to be NASCAR-worthy. This restriction may have become too severe to both NASCAR and Detroit. New looks were needed to keep up interest. The brand identification of cars was still important to the manufacturers.

If Earnhardt won in a Chevrolet, that was still free ink in the sports pages, and sporty model street versions were still in demand.

Collectors quickly scooped up the 200 SS models and Chevy had a race-winning combination with Earnhardt at the wheel.

Once again, his aggressive driving style surfaced as drivers and car owners commented on his no-holds-barred style. Dale just dusted off his "Aw shucks" grin along with his equally dusty stories about watching his daddy race with the likes of Junior Johnson on dirt, way back when, and everyone who didn't have to share the track with him at 200 miles per hour nodded, chuckled, and printed the tales again for his growing number of fans. He caught more than his share of boos from the grandstands as he would spin out a competitor by hooking a rear bumper and giving the steering wheel a twitch. But those same fist-shakers were on their feet cheering at the end if he was in or close to the lead. Most of his fans identified with him, looking for a way to get to the front no matter the means—as long as no one got seriously hurt.

The Busch Clash wasn't Earnhardt's only victory at Daytona's Speed Week. Still piloting the Monte Carlo SS, he managed a one-second win over Geoff Bodine driving a standard Monte Carlo and Rusty Wallace in a Pontiac Grand Prix 2+2. That was his second 125-mile qualifier win, the first coming back in 1983. This SS car was virtually identical to the coupe he had used to win the Clash four days earlier except it was roughly one inch narrower. The new Chevy fast-back slanting rear-window design was definitely the car to beat, but its air flow over the roof and spoiler made it difficult to follow in a draft. Other shops running the Monte Carlo SS were having a hard time setting up their suspension springs to accommodate the new design. As for Earnhardt, he turned 48 minutes and 56 seconds of very intense work into $22,000.

Yet, the big race—the Daytona 500—was denied him once again and for the most mundane failure—he ran out of gas. But that was to be the only ripple in the smooth sailing that was the 1986 season if you don't count the February dustup at the Miller High Life 400 at Richmond, Virginia.

Earnhardt not only didn't win it, he was the focal point of a lot of finger pointing from NASCAR, a raging Junior Johnson, and many of his fellow drivers. Dale had clipped the right rear bumper of Darrell Waltrip rushing into turn three. That tap sent Waltrip spinning into a steel guardrail and snared four other cars in a whirling, tire-screeching, clatter-crash tangle that gutted the leaders in that lap. NASCAR jumped high and landed hard, leveling a $5,000 fine on Earnhardt for overaggressive driving. It was later reduced, but the $3,000 still smarted and added to the judgment that Earnhardt would do anything to win a race—and to anyone.

Earnhardt and Childress took their hot Chevy to Darlington for the TranSouth 500. From the time that the GM mill churned the blue and yellow racer out onto the asphalt until it rolled into victory lane at the end, he had led 335 of the 367 laps and became the 11th different winner of the last 11 NASCAR Winston Cup races—proving the wisdom of leveling the field.

Almost everyone spent the race chasing Earnhardt, who kept up a sizzling pace that even had Childress nervous. Later, Earnhardt told reporters every time he slowed down, he lost his preferred line through the curves, so he felt better just keeping the hammer down all the way and the Childress-prepared car never faltered. By the end of the race, only he and pursuer Darrell Waltrip in another Chevy were on the same lap. He had passed all the other racers and finished with an average speed of 128.994 miles per hour around the 1.366 mile track. The victory brought him closer to point leader Waltrip by a margin of 952 to 1,000 points.

With one Winston Cup trophy on the shelf, Childress-Earnhardt stalked the field once again at the North Wilkesboro Speedway on April 20 for the First Union 400. Earnhardt had started on this short—0.625 mile—track 16 times without a win, but the 17th start was charmed as he won by two car lengths over Ricky Rudd in a Bud Moore Thunderbird. Rudd had pushed Earnhardt hard all day, but in the end got beaten due to a fast pit stop by the Childress crew while Rudd's crew was sabotaged by a failed air hose on the socket wrench used to remove one of the tires. Earnhardt's Chevy bellowed out of the pits into the lead.

Rudd hammered the gas, driving recklessly trying to catch Earnhardt and give him a little bumper tag like he had received so many times, but he couldn't catch the blue and yellow car as more than 29,000 fans cheered their favorite around the short track.

And so the 1986 NASCAR season went. In May, Earnhardt went into the Coca-Cola 600 at the Charlotte Motor Speedway in Harrisburg, North Carolina, with his car handling poorly and with no confidence for a win. With 100 laps remaining, the pit crew finally worked out the combination of wedge in the springs and stagger with the tires and suddenly the car gripped its line with confidence. After a battle of pit stops, Earnhardt took over the lead with 16 laps left and held it.

Charlotte was again the site of a win for Earnhardt as he took the Oakwood Homes 500 despite tire problems throughout. Later, he condemned fans who tossed empty bottles and cans onto the track, telling reporters it was like "driving in the parking lot."

In Atlanta for the Atlanta Journal 500, Earnhardt clinched his second Winston Cup Series Championship. He broke the track record with an average speed of 152.523 miles per hour, leading the race for 162 laps. Bill Elliott had grabbed the pole position with a speed of 172.905 miles per hour but could not get the job done in traffic. Earnhardt's point lead was such that he had the win sewn up even if he had come in 26th because Waltrip's best finish would have been 39th after a blown engine.

Earnhardt showed no signs of stopping as he piled 11 Winston Cup trophies on his cabinet shelves and then a third Winston Series Championship piloting the blue and yellow Wrangler Childress Monte Carlo SS. His final win at Richmond, taking the Wrangler Indigo 400, boosted his winnings for the year 1987 to $1,231,920. Besides the championship, Earnhardt created another bit of lore that remains attached to his career to this day.

About halfway through the 1987 season, he was booming around the Charlotte Speedway course trying to find some air to get clear of the pack. He suddenly found himself involved in a three-way collision of sorts. Bill Elliott, Geoff Bodine, and Earnhardt all came together in the same space resulting in a spectacular spinning, smoking, tire-scuffing, metal-shearing crash that propelled Earnhardt off the track and onto the grassy verge that borders the asphalt. Instead of throwing in his cards and calling it a day, Earnhardt floored the gas and kept going, sending clods of green sod from beneath his rear wheels and managing to pass other cars before turning back up and onto the racing surface. Of course, the officials went purple over that fistful of violations and fined Earnhardt, Bodine, and Elliott. But in racing legend that ramble through the wilderness was made immortal as The Pass in the Grass.

An era ended for Wrangler's "tough customer" in 1988 as a new sponsor joined Childress Racing. General Motors had announced a new set of maintenance programs for their service shops under the banner of "Mr. Goodwrench." To make this transition even greater than just slapping on a new decal, in a special press event a new car was uncovered for the cameras. An all-black Chevrolet Monte Carlo SS emblazoned with the slanted number three gave birth to yet another name for The Intimidator. To many of his fans, Dale Earnhardt became The Man in Black. His car would wear that signature color for the rest of his career.

Some of his rivals chose the nickname Darth Vader, tying him to the evil destroyer of worlds—who would as soon spin you into the wall if you failed to let him pass. He took the Chevy to victory lane three times in 1988. He might have done better, but the NASCAR teams got caught up in tire wars.

Drivers' lives and livelihood hang on where the rubber meets the road, especially at 200 miles per hour. A team can spend a million dollars on tires in one season—and do so gladly considering the investment riding on the four small footprints those tires offer the driver to maintain control at high speeds. Back in the dirt-track days, Ralph Earnhardt started out carving tread into his own tires with different cuts for each track. Later, he tested Firestone tires for Humpy Wheeler as the tire companies realized the huge market stock car racing offered for their products.

Due to the high speeds and expected wear, racing tires are usually made of a harder rubber compound than street tires. On modern asphalt tracks, they are also slick—have no treads—so in case of rain, the races are usually halted. Goodyear chose 1987 to introduce new radial tires to racing. Today, radials are standard equipment on all showroom cars, but in 1987, bias-ply tires were the norm. They were subject to shredding when worn and wore out quickly at racing speeds. The new Goodyear radials were bolted on the cars running the 71st Indianapolis 500 Race held on May 24, 1987.

Almost at once the air was filled with spinning, crashing cars during qualifying and practice. An unusually high 25 crashes tore a great chunk out of the field of competitors and emptied a lot of spare-parts bins before the race even started. Crews had to frantically reset suspensions to correct for the new tires. With parting shots of "A lousy suspension can't be helped by a great tire!" Goodyear went back to the drawing board.

Following that horror, NASCAR was advised that maybe more than one supplier should be used to supply tires to their cars. NASCAR chose to try this theory on the upcoming 1988 Sprint Cup Series. The Hoosier Racing Tire Corporation, a small Indiana company, found itself competing against the giant from Akron, Ohio—Goodyear. Hoosier had supplied tires to Late Model, Sprint, and Sportsman races on short tracks, so it was not a complete newcomer. In 1987 Hoosier had put tires on Busch Series cars as well and experienced the full superspeedway trial. But in 1988, the head-to-head competition for tire supremacy reached the Winston Cup Series big leagues.

Hoosier tires were cheaper and made of a softer compound and many teams opted for them. The major shops, however, remained loyal to Goodyear. The major shops stood in their pits and watched the Hoosier-shod drivers wheel away with victories in the first 16 races of the season. At the March 6, 1988, Goodwrench 500, for example, spectators at the Rockingham, North Carolina, Motor Speedway watched Neil Bonnett roar from 30th place on the starting grid to win. He trounced the 2nd-place Lake Speed by a full second. Bonnett, Speed, and the next two finishers all wore Hoosier tires.

What to do? Goodyear gritted its teeth and waited for Hoosier to run out of steam.

Chaos was common in pit row. Hoosier's softer tire compounds seemed to be faster, but they blew, as did Goodyear's as the tire giant tried to give the drivers what was demanded. Crews stocked both brands in great mounds of rubber behind the pits, sometimes switching back and forth in a race as everyone hunted for the magic formula. Meanwhile, drivers were soaring off into walls, turning graceful machines into shredded ruins, and binding up bruises with sticky tape. Goodyear representatives chewed their knuckles as champion drivers ended upside down in the infield or painted a jagged smear down the turn three wall. At the Charlotte Motor Speedway during the World 600, Rick Wilson, Davey Allison, Harry Gant, and Neil Bonnett were all carted off to the hospital following tire failures. Goodyear, fearing an even greater slaughter, withdrew its tires, leaving the field to gingerly race on shod with the soft, bias-ply Hoosiers.

Worst of all, the teams were going broke trying to stock both brands of tires. A million here, a million there, pretty soon everyone was discussing serious money. Something had to be done.

NASCAR was bound by antitrust laws which forbade them from dumping one manufacturer or the other. Fortunately for Goodyear, their tires held up though the second half of the season winning 20 races.

The Earnhardt/Childress team finished out of 1st place for the 1988 season, but roared into the 1989 tournaments with enthusiasm aboard four Goodyear radial tires—reintroduced after the Indianapolis 500 nightmare. This tire bolted onto the all-black machine wearing the slanted number three was a fast, durable world-beater. And where better to show off the tire than the opening superspeedway race of the season, the Daytona 500.

Dale strapped on the four new tires and bellowed out of the pits and onto the Daytona track looking to blow away the competition. He drove into the wall and smeared his car across the track. Then Bill Elliott boomed out onto the asphalt and went screeching into the concrete barrier, breaking his wrist in the bargain. Goodyear sent its trucks around to the pits and garages, withdrawing its tires from the Daytona 500.

On April 16, 1989, running in the First Union 400 at North Wilkesboro Raceway, Goodyear radials lagged behind the Hoosiers when it came to sheer speed. But as the race wore on, the Akron tires proved better at sustaining high speed as the Hoosiers needed replacing. Dale Earnhardt on Goodyear radials won his 35th race and started that season's campaign, which would see him win four more times, but he came up short to Rusty Wallace for the Championship.

Goodyear had proved the value of the radial tire and in May the Hoosier Tire Corporation gave up the racing-tire business since they did not manufacture a radial tire. The other reason was economics. In one of their draconian rulings, NASCAR solidified Goodyear's position as sole tire supplier by requiring suppliers to provide enough tires for every car in the race—about 2,000 tires. That was beyond the capabilities of the small Hoosier Corporation. They tried again six years later with a radial tire design but were defeated again by NASCAR's inflexible rules.[1]

In 1990, Earnhardt drove to nine wins and his fourth Winston Cup Series Championship. He was in a groove. He had long ago moved past the identity "Ralph's kid." He had carved himself a successful career in racing and with Teresa built an empire that eventually included souvenir merchandise, racing associated businesses, a car dealership, a 400-acre farm near Mooresville, North Carolina, and a race shop of his own in an ultramodern complex just outside that town that was so large it was nicknamed the Garage Mahal.

His life outside the racetrack had become a southern boy's dream. During the brief off-season, he enjoyed hunting and fishing on his own property as well as on land leased in South Carolina and Montana. He roamed his farm working at odd jobs: clearing trees with his bulldozer, looking after his horses and 200 head of beef cattle, or stopping by the chicken house where thousands of eggs a day were produced by his 30,000 chickens. He pitched hay and got his hands dirty when he wished, but there was a staff at the farm to keep it running and provide day-to-day maintenance.

But one part of this ideal life was missing. Over the years, Dale had discovered a life-long friend in Neil Bonnett, a fellow driver. It is unusual for drivers to have close friends among the competitors they race against each week. It's not like any other sport where, at the end of the contest, everyone adjourns to the clubhouse bar or meets with the wives for a dinner party. More often, it was some trash talk and needling in the garage, a beer or soft drink to cut the dust, and everybody went their separate ways. Over the years, most of the high-level drivers had a big, boxy recreational vehicle to call home when they weren't needed in the garage or on the track. Except for the crew members, the race season was a solitary time for the drivers when they weren't glad-handing the sponsors, signing autographs, or making paid public appearances.

Having Teresa at the races was a bonus for Dale and when the kids showed up from military school on vacation break, he enjoyed their company too. Then, when Teresa gave birth to Taylor Nicole on December 20, 1988, Dale had competition for Teresa's attention. Taylor was her baby and became the focus of the family.

Dale and Neil had met in the 1970s when Neil was part of the Alabama gang along with the Allison brothers. Dale was five years younger and had only two years of undistinguished racing under his belt. By the end of the 1970s, they were both up-and-coming hot dogs and neither one could tell which one was the sidekick, so they just left it at that.

Their best times together were passed hiking down forest trails on their way to a pair of deer stands lugging either a compound bow or a scoped rifle. They were equally at home casting a crank bait to the edge of some lily pads and twitching it back waiting for a largemouth bass to strike. They had the kind of friendship that enjoyed the large silences too. Neil was forgiving of Dale's gentle bully personality, the need to roughhouse and intimidate people for the fun of embarrassing them. That was Dale's style, just like on the track. Neil was a softer counterpart, and they complemented each other.

Neil Bonnett had become an important sounding board for Dale as they hunted and fished together or just hung out when they were not racing. Bonnett became family. On April 1, 1990, Neil crashed and came out of the accident with periods of amnesia and dizziness. He was determined to continue racing and continued sporadically until February 11, 1994, when, during a qualifying lap, his tire blew, putting him head-first into the wall. Dale was stricken by Neil's death. It was a wound similar to that left by the passing of a favorite pet, someone who loved you warts and all without reservation, the kind of friend whom you counted on to side you in any scrape. And now Dale's flank was unprotected.

In the '90s, his winnings climbed to $3.6 million, but his annual income climbed to over $40 million a year when all his other investments were factored in, according to the *Business Journal of Charlotte*. The money he raked in from his signature, face, and that slanted number three on the side of the black car made whatever prize money he won in a race irrelevant.

Added to the list were all the rich boy toys too: the 77-foot Hatteras yacht christened Sunday Money moored at Daytona, Florida, as part of the fleet owned by a loose collection of racers and racing businessmen who make up the NASCAR Yacht Club. For basic transportation, he bought a Learjet 31 in 1990. It was registered to Champion Air LLC, a company with the same address in Mooresville, North Carolina, as Dale Earnhardt Inc.[2] For shorter hops below 51,000 feet and slower than 594 miles per hour, he climbed aboard a Bell 407 helicopter.

All the trappings of success were his and Teresa's as the silver, gold, crystal, and polished wood trophies filled the Trophy Room at DEI. But the man had a lot of catching up to do as his new life surrounded him. Especially with Neil gone, he had to turn around and be a father to his three children: Kerry, Kelley, and Dale Jr., as well as baby Taylor Nicole.

His relationship with his own father had been a mix of respect and resentment, of looking for affection and affirmation, and he had received only grudging approval from the man who wanted better things for his son. Now Dale had to grow up alongside his children and find out who they were.

## NOTES

1. Scene Daily, "History Shows NASCAR Doing just Fine with Goodyear as One Tire Manufacturer," http://www.scenedaily.com/news/articles/print/History_shows_NASCAR_doing_just_fine_with_one_tire_manufacturer.html.

2. JetLit, "Teresa Earnhardt's Learjet 31," http://www.jetjit.com/teresa-earnhardts-learjet-31/.

# Chapter 16

# INHERITING THE CHALICE

Dale Earnhardt's children grew up on two levels. The last child, Taylor Nicole, only knew the perks of wealth and the fussy attention of her father and mother. For example, during his travels, Dale discovered a Chevrolet Corvette built in 1988—Taylor's birth year—and had it completely restored. He gave her the car as a present and at age 12 she learned to drive it with him riding shotgun.[1] He was proud of all his children and frequently bragged about their accomplishments. As he moved into his 40s, he might have seen himself as he remembered his father. But Dale had everything a man could desire instead of a lingering debt paid off month by month as his father's small racing purses kept Dale and his brothers and sister in shoes and food, as well as with a roof over their heads. That life had aged Ralph Earnhardt beyond his years because he was a man who balanced his responsibilities with his need for self-respect. Like his father, Dale wanted a better life for his children than he had known at their age.

It wasn't that he had a hard life, but he had defied his parents' demands that he get an education and not end up a linthead at Cannon mill, or even a dirt-track race driver living from purse to purse. His first three children, all born before he was 23 years old, were all raised in poor homes and trailers. His first son, Kerry, eventually left to live with his mother when she divorced Dale. Kelley and Dale Jr., his sons with Brenda Gee, stayed closer to him, but he was absent from their lives as he struggled to make enough money for their needs and for his race cars. He began living his father's life all over again. In 1979, he was away racing when faulty wiring in their old mill-owned company house caused a fire that destroyed the building, and the children moved in with Dale in Mooresville while Brenda got settled once again.

Dale had finally begun to see some real money as he drove on the Winston Cup Circuit, but the racing season kept him constantly on the road. His only contact with Kelley and Dale Jr. was by telephone. When they did have time together, it was either frantic and fun, or Dale was exhausted and half asleep in his recliner with a beer in front of the television. When Dale Jr. was six, his father taught him to water ski and then there was the go-cart, a small gasoline-powered racer built low to the ground. As their father always seemed to be on the go, they tried their best to keep up.

When Dale married Teresa in 1982, she accompanied him on the road, leaving the kids in the charge of hired nannies. Dale Jr. was small for his age and found school to be both humiliating and a grind. Kelley was his rock and friend when he needed to talk. He began to give his parents a hard time with attitude and rebellion. At this time, Dale's star was rising in NASCAR. He didn't dare reduce his schedule of races because prize money still made up the bulk of his income. But his son had discipline problems and needed a firm hand. Closing his ears to their whining and carrying on, Dale enrolled Kelley and Dale Jr. in the Oak Ridge Military Academy in Oak Ridge, North Carolina.

Clad in military gray, the Earnhardt children marched off to become cadets and face day-to-day regimentation and structured lives that their father had never known. Later, they would admit that though they were horrified at the idea of military school at the time, they eventually appreciated the result of the enforced rules and teamwork training.

After two years, Dale Jr. returned to Mooresville Senior High School where he surrounded himself with a group of close, trustworthy friends. With his attitude buffed down, he and his father were more comfortable together. About this time, his older brother Kerry came to live with the Earnhardts and a bond grew between the boys as their interest in racing developed. Kerry was the hot dog while Dale Jr. remained cautious. He had first driven a car at age 12 sitting alongside his father on a deserted highway, and from there worked on the engine of Ralph Earnhardt's old go-cart, but he stayed away from competition driving.

Kerry and Dale Jr. spent time scrounging in junk yards until they selected a down-at-the-heels Chevy Monte Carlo. Together, they restored it and joined by their sister Kelley, they raced the old junker at Concord Motorsports Park. When pressed, they had to admit, it was Kelley who was the best driver of the three.

Dale encouraged his kids' racing motorcycles, horses, ATVs, anything that would go up and down the roads of their new farm, but only if their schoolwork was up-to-date. One important holdover from Dale's grow-ing up under Ralph's mentoring stayed with the Earnhardt family: there was no free ride. If the three kids wanted to race, they paid their own way. They earned the money to buy a car and parts to make it race-wor-thy. This is as hard for a father to enforce as it is for the offspring to ac-cept. It is easy for a dad to make a few phone calls and open a few doors, but where do those perks leave the racer in the eyes of his competitors and of the fans, most of whom worked hard to even pay for tickets to the race. And Dale Earnhardt had worked hard for the success he finally enjoyed.

Dale Jr. took the step into NASCAR Late Model racing at age 19—younger than most of the drivers on the circuit—and had a good first two years on the short tracks driving older cars. He won twice and stayed in the top five in more than half his races. That was hardly a financial success story, so, like Kerry and Kelley, Dale Jr. went to work for Dale Earn-hardt Inc. The business that started out in a garage had grown through li-censed memorabilia, investments, race car building and selling, showroom car dealerships, and Dale's ability to consistently drive at the top level of competition.

For Dale Jr. that meant starting out, not at the top in administration, but with a broom in his hand as a floor sweeper and horse stall mucker. "All I heard from my dad," he said, "was 'You got to start at the bottom, sweeping floors.'" He added, "And I said, 'I'm going straight to the driver's seat.' He'd laugh, but I meant it."[2] Scrimping and saving, Dale Jr. fielded a car and a crew at the track in Myrtle Beach, South Carolina, in June 1996 and pulled out a 13th place finish. The run was all Earnhardt. Vet-erans who watched Dale Jr. run remarked on the uncanny similarity to his grandfather's driving style.

Taking the next big step, Dale Jr. traveled up to the Michigan Speed-way in 1997 for a go at the Detroit Gasket 200, where he managed a 7th place finish, his best place out of seven races that year.

By 1998, Dale Jr. had run and won, run and wrecked in many races. He had also discovered that his failures, as well as his best moments behind the wheel, were understood by his father. That year would be a big one for both Earnhardt and son. DEI decided to field a Busch Series car and Dale Sr. asked Dale Jr. to test it. It is customary to ask the potential driver of a new car to test it before he runs it in a race. Dale Sr. took his sweet time down to the wire, never hinting that Dale Jr. was the new car's pilot. It wasn't until the name decals for the side of the car came into the shop that Dale Jr. had confirmation that he would indeed be driving the new racer. He took that new car out onto the Daytona track and roared into the Busch Series Napa Auto Parts 300. He managed to wreck the car and finished 37th.

But the Daytona Speed Week of 1998 still belonged to the Earnhardts. Nineteen times Dale Sr. had gone to the well at the Daytona 500 race and came up empty. He had lost the race every way possible from running out of gas to hitting a seagull. The Daytona 500 was the Super Bowl of NAS-CAR racing—the start of the season—the big event that every driver on the Winston Cup Circuit wanted to win and needed to win to cement superstar status. He had just come off the 1997 season without winning a single race. Maybe the magic was gone; the fire that had driven him had settled into ash.

Before the race, Dale Sr. was making the usual sponsor rounds before settling into his racing mode and shutting down to focus on the job at hand. A little girl in a wheelchair had wanted an autograph from The Man in Black so he obliged with a smile for the cameras. She gave him a lucky penny to carry with him during the race. He gave it to his crew chief who had it glued to the car's dashboard. This time, the luck would be all Earnhardt's.

The grandstands were filled with his fans. Black flags flew emblazoned with slanted number threes. Red hats were everywhere. People waved holding up three fingers. The horrific din rose above the superspeedway as the green flag dropped and from that moment, Earnhardt took command. But that meant nothing in this race. He had led before only to experience disaster in the final laps. He pushed the big Chevy hard circling the oval at an average speed of 172.712 miles per hour, always keeping that long black hood at or near the front of the pack. It was the only way he knew how to run. He had won a total of seven Winston Cup Series Championships—tying Richard Petty's record—with his foot mashed to the floor and off the brakes. The new kid, Jeff Gordon, was in hot pursuit. On the last lap of the race, four cars tangled, bringing out the caution flag at the finish line—together with the white flag signifying one lap remaining. Whoever reached those two flags first would win the race. Earnhardt flew down turn four. Gordon had dropped out with a blown cylinder, but Wallace and Labonte were hot on his heels. He jinked around Rick Mast's lapped car and both Labonte and Wallace swapped paint trying to find room to challenge. With the throttle wide open, Dale Earnhardt blasted across the finish line, winner of the Daytona 500, and the grandstands exploded with cheers as a capacity crowd on their feet yelled themselves hoarse, hugged, wept, and felt themselves sitting beside their Man in Black as he circled the track with his hand raised outside the driver's window.

Along pit row, virtually every crew man, owner, spare driver, sponsor rep, and NASCAR official stood in a line to slap that outstretched hand as a sign of respect for the man who—as he said later to the press—"Got that monkey off my back!" The day of that race was truly the best day of Dale Earnhardt's racing life, and he shared it with his wife and kids, with Taylor Nicole giving him his traditional winner's kiss on the cheek.

The following year, Dale Earnhardt Jr., following his father's example, founded his own company, JR Motorsports, as a base for his own racing program and attendant investments.

The year 2000 found Dale Earnhardt still suited up and finishing the season at Talladega on October 15. He was pushing 50 and carried himself more like a car owner, a well-barbered businessman than a lean, hungry fire-eater. The creases in his face and neck had settled into a permanent geography, the lines and folds of a man who smiles a lot and has squinted into his share of sunrises. But those restless eyes still missed nothing, and he found time as he headed toward the pit to sign a few autographs, scrawl his name on a T-shirt or hat, and shake a few tentatively offered hands. He had a few words for Danny "Chocolate" Myers, the huge gasman in his crew that heaved the big gas can over the wall during pit stops. Like Richard Childress, Myers and the rest of the crew had been key members of the winning team for the past 10 years and seven Winston Championships, tying the mark set by "The King," Richard Petty. For them, the fall day in Alabama was another day at the office.

NASCAR, in its wisdom, had designated this Winston 500 to be a restrictor plate race. The organization had been working hard and testing endlessly to create a sweeping aerodynamic package that applied to all the cars and was enforced by templates applied to the exterior surfaces during tech inspection before the race to assure conformity. The ground clearance had been raised to reduce the vacuum-like effect binding the car to the track. Also added was an extended flange to the car's roof called a wickerbill or Gurney Flap, named after the racing legend Dan Gurney, who borrowed the idea from an airplane design. The idea was to further slow the car to allow passing on the high-speed tracks. Now, with that boat anchor bolted on, NASCAR dragged out the little plates that were sealed in place beneath the carburetors, restricting the air flow and reducing the engine's power. Dale hated restrictor-plate racing. Most of the drivers shared his dislike, claiming it was like watching the parking lot circle the track—one big mass of cars sometimes running three and four abreast with nobody able to break away, sucked in together by the unbreakable draft—boring.

But the fans loved the track and the spectacle. An MTV camera crew wandered around the infield picking up color shots, and NASCAR was nervous about the image of southern stock car racing being broadcast based on the rowdy, fun-loving, bare-chested, tattoo-decorated, beer-bottle waving crowd. The running gag was "What has 40 legs and 10 teeth? The ticket line for the Talladega infield."

One factor in the race was not boring: Dale and Dale Jr. were running in the same race. There was a lot of tension over the new rules, new tacked-on metal, and the dangerous reputation of the track. Many drivers headed for the Motor Racing Outreach chapel after the drivers' meeting and listened to Dale Beaver give the sermon.

Race time approached. High above the track were the spotters, every team has at least one, armed with binoculars and a multichannel radio, one of which is hooked to the driver's helmet in each car. The spotters are the driver's and pit manager's main communication link to what is happening on the track—especially valuable on a long one like Talladega.

Dale slid into the black machine, strapped in—and loosened the strap just enough so he could assume his leaning-against-the-door driving position—a habit he'd been warned about by just about everybody.[3] Over his helmet radio, he said howdy to the pits and his own spotter, tripped the toggle switches on the dashboard, and with a rumble that vibrates the viscera, the big engine kicked over and the black Mr. Goodwrench Chevy headed out onto the track, forming up with the other racers for their day at the office.

Forty-two feet simultaneously tramped the gas pedals as the cars tried to stretch out from the mob boiling down out of turn three for the green flag and then they were racing. Dale Jr. tore into the lead for the first lap, but the pack was close behind. Lap after lap saw lead changes and Dale Jr. found himself working with his dad as they diced through the crowd staying within striking distance of the lead. But there were 40 other drivers who wanted to win this race real bad and neither Earnhardt could make much headway. The top 31 cars were in a knot that passed in two seconds. Fenders rubbed, squealed, and clattered, while steering wheels whipped with every touch. Rear ends got loosey-goosey as the track slicked up.

To break the draft sucking everyone along at nightmare speeds, Dale Jr. pulled up hard behind his dad and hammered the rear end of the black Chevy. He did it again and punched the car forward. It's called bump drafting and is used by teammates to help acceleration into the straights. On the sideline, Teresa could not see what was happening as her husband and son were wheeling around that mad oval. She'd seen it many times before with Dale, but now, both . . .

At the pits, Dale Jr. braked into the painted box just right and the bodies of his crew swarmed over the wall flailing hoses. The Number Eight car tilted as two Goodyear Eagles were bolted in place with a piercing whine of the wrenches. The air stank of fuel as a few gallons were sloshed into the tank. The car dropped. There was a hand signal. The pit lane was checked. The gas was mashed and the car gunned back into the chaos. He was out in 7.91 seconds and held his lead. Behind him, Labonte gave him a love tap and they ran first and second with eight laps to go.

Suddenly, they were not alone. Mike Skinner back in 3rd made a run on Labonte. Now, every driver who was free of the dreaded pack made their run and flew toward the leaders. Dale Jr. couldn't see his dad anywhere. He and Labonte fired through into the last two laps at the head of the jam and then, in the rearview mirror, surging through like a freight train, came the Man in Black. Tucked in behind him was Ken Wallace, drafting just as close as he dared, upping the speed of both cars.

Dale had worked his way from 18th with less than five laps to go. Now Dale Jr. had run out of options. He hurtled into the next turn getting bumped-drafted by his teammate Labonte, but now the bumps were causing his rear end to fishtail. Traveling the length of a football field a second, he could tough it out and either miss the wall, or cause the biggest wreck in NASCAR history. His third option was to lift. His dad's one constant instruction drummed into him since he first sat behind a race car steering wheel was "Never lift! Never Lift! Never lift!"

Dale Jr. lifted his foot from the gas and saved the car. He also plummeted back to 14th place. His dad exploded past, burst into the clear, and won the race, towing Kenny Wallace behind him. As Dale Jr. wrote later, "He kicked our asses."[4]

## NOTES

1. Lee Spencer, Sporting News.com, *Earnhardt's Last Race a Selfless Act*, February 18, 2001, http://www.sportingnews.com/archives/earnhardt/selfless.html.

2. Mark Stewart, *Dale Earnhardt Jr.: Driven by Destiny* (Brookfield, CT: Millbrook Press, 2003), pp. 16–17.

3. Marshall Brooks, interview with the author, Concord, NC., October 16, 2008.

4. Dale Earnhardt Jr. with Jade Gurss, *Driver #8* (New York: Warner Books, 2002), pp. 250–260.

# Chapter 17

# THE LEGACY

Today, NASCAR sits at the same table with the NFL and the NBA. It generates billions of dollars entertaining millions of fans from coast to coast as stock car racing has spread across the United States like a rash. The world created inside each of the NASCAR tracks is like none other in sports: the booming noise, the standing crowds, blaring music and, at the end when the winner is crowned, champagne sprayed over the assembled infield and pit folk. American stock car racing is garish, loud, and physical. The cars look alike and serve as shameless billboards while the drivers (white, male) fit a pattern that would not be out of place modeling men's suits on a fashion runway. The southern culture permeates the sport to its roots and below the Mason-Dixon Line proudly proclaims its blue-collar testosterone-soaked heritage beneath fluttering Confederate flags. African Americans will need a sudden success story like Michael Jordan or Tiger Woods to break loose sponsor money for winning teams. Women are better off as fearless hard chargers like Danica Patrick continue to go round and round smoking donuts on that glass ceiling.

But for all its bloated success and hype, NASCAR has shed light on a unique collection of very brave race car drivers who for 10 months out of the year make their living in the world's most dangerous and demanding sport. The best of them have finely tuned athleticism, engineering smarts, business sense, and personal self-confidence that rank high up the scale. NASCAR gave these gifted people a way to stretch their talents that is better than running moonshine over dirt roads in pitch dark.

Even considering NASCAR's tremendous legacy, the last words go to the drivers. The Earnhardts are just one of the mini-dynasties like the Pettys, the Flocks, the Allisons, and the new generation of individuals: Gordon, Stewart, Martin, Waltrip, Harvick, Labonte, Kyle Busch, and the others. The Earnhardts—Ralph, Dale, and Dale Jr. —have spanned the entire panorama from the '50s to the present and now Kerry Earnhardt is running in the Craftsman Truck Series. For this narrative they will have the last word.

## FEBRUARY 18, 2001

The crowd is on their feet at the Daytona 500 under a Florida sun and two Earnhardts are in the last lap. Dale Jr. runs 2nd and Dale Sr. sits back at 3rd. In the lead is Darrell Waltrip's son Michael. Fans of the Man in Black can't believe what they are seeing. As the cars blast through the front stretch and reach up into the banking of turns one and two, Dale Earnhardt is not storming toward the lead. He is holding back, blocking cars behind him from gaining on the two leaders. He's never done this before. Win at all costs. Second just means "first loser," those are the Intimidator's guiding principles. But he's hanging back protecting the two leaders, both driving cars he owns. Darrell Waltrip is in the broadcast booth, on his feet, cheering his son along over the microphone. The cheers blend into a continuous roar.

And then Sterling Martin's car gets loose and its bumper taps the rear of Dale Earnhardt's Chevy high on the outside of the track. The Chevy breaks loose, its rear end swinging toward the center of the track. Martin's front end plows forward into the passenger side of the Number Three car and in the space of a few feet, the Chevy impacts the wall with such force that the passenger side window blows out. Deeply wounded, the car rolls backwards down into the infield tangled with Martin's car and trailing smoke.

All eyes are on the two leaders who howl across the finish line, Michael Waltrip followed by Dale Jr., and most of the crowd yahoos and waves, but some keep looking back up the track where the safety crews have driven to the crumpled black Chevy lying deflated and silent. Flashing lights and a flurry of activity surround Earnhardt's car and then gradually the activity dies down. In the broadcast booth, Waltrip has seen his boy cross the finish line. Grinning, he looks back up the track. "How's Dale?" he asks no one in particular. "He's alright isn't he?" His big smile fades.[1]

Dale Earnhardt died from a broken neck caused by hammering his head against the steering wheel on impact with the concrete wall. He was killed instantly. The void his passing left in American stock car racing persists to this day. The fans won't let it go. He was one of them. In the words of the late automobile writer Kenneth Purdy on the death of Alfonso de Portago, the premier road racer of all time:

"A dead lion's a greater thing than a live mouse."

Trying to keep himself together, the week after his father's funeral, Dale Jr. ran in the Dura Lube 400 and promptly crashed on the first lap. That was the start of a five-month depression. He had become so absorbed into his father's world, NASCAR's world, that memories were everywhere. Eventually, the season returned to Daytona for the Pepsi 400.

There weren't many dry eyes around the superspeedway as Dale Jr. accelerated into the parade lap, passing the spot where the skid marks remained from his father's last race. The green flag dropped and, like his daddy before him, he had business to take care of. By the end of the race, the fans knew they had another Earnhardt to cheer and to stalk for autographs, and whose hats and T-shirts they could buy. Maybe he didn't play quite so rough on the track and instead of hunting, fishing, and horseback riding, he preferred video games, stereo music, and partying with friends. When the checkered flag dropped on his grandfather Ralph's Number Eight, they knew Dale Jr. was a winner and that's all that counted.

## EPILOGUE

Today, Dale Earnhardt Inc. still lives in the Garage Mahal just outside Mooresville, North Carolina. For fans, it is a mirrored glass shrine worthy of a pilgrimage. It features cabinets filled with Dale Earnhardt's trophies and memorabilia: saddles, hats, matching luggage, belt buckles, and in frames on the wall, racing uniforms from different periods of his career. A showroom behind thick glass displays a collection of NASCAR racers, and some of Dale's cars are shown up close and touchable. The gift shop is impressive. Teresa Earnhardt now runs the company, but Dale Jr. no longer drives for DEI.

He left the company in 2007 to drive for Rick Hendrick Motorsports, a decision confirmed in 2008. His manager is his sister, Kelley Earnhardt-Elledge. Former rivals are now teammates like Jeff Gordon, who Dale Sr. referred to sarcastically as Wonderboy because of the young man's accomplishments at such as early age—typifying the new breed of drivers. NASCAR continues to be a family sport that started with Bill France and his wife Anne, who stopped their car on a stretch of sandy beach in Florida and took a look around.

## NOTE

1. *Dale*, DVD, directed by Rory Karpf and Mike Viney; (Charlotte, NC: NASCAR Images and CMT Films, 2007).

Gillispie, Tom. *I Remember Dale Earnhardt*. Nashville, TN: Cumberland House, 2001.

Golenbock, Peter. *NASCAR Confidential*. St. Paul, MN: MBI Publishing, 2004.

Granger, Gene. "Yarborough Fails to Rattle Sophomore," In *The Earnhardt Collection: Because Winning Matters*. Chicago, IL: Triumph Books and Charlotte, NC: Street & Smith's Sports, 2006.

Hembree, Mike. *NASCAR: The Definitive History of American Sport*. New York: Harper Entertainment, 2000.

JetJit. "Teresa Earnhardt's Learjet 31." http://www.jetjit.com/teresa-earnhardts-learjet-31/.

London, Grey. "Following the Earnhardt Connection." *Concord-Kannapolis Daily Independent*. (Kannapolis, NC).

Mane, Kenny. *The Dale Earnhardt Story*. New York: Hyperion, 2004.

Martin, Mark. *NASCAR for Dummies, 2nd Edition*. Hoboken, NJ: Wiley, 2004.

Menzer, Joe. *The Wildest Ride: A History of NASCAR*. New York: Simon & Schuster, 2001.

Mike's NASCAR Page. "A Brief History of NASCAR." http://www.mindspring.com/~mike.wicks/nascarhistory2.html.

*NASCAR Record & Fact Book*. St. Louis, MO: Sporting News Books, 2007.

One Bad Wheel. "Martinsville Speedway." http://www.onebadwheel.com/martinsville-speedway-nascar/track/.

Purdy, Ken. *Ken Purdy's Book of Automobiles*. New York: Playboy Press, 1972.

Sechler, Ethel. "Champ's Mother is Very Proud of All Her Children." *Concord-Kannapolis Daily Independent*. (Kannapolis, NC), October 3, 1993.

Singer, Mark P. and Ryan L. Sumner. *Auto Racing in Charlotte and the Carolina Piedmont*. Charleston, SC: Arcadia Press, 2003.

Smith, D. Brian. "Bob Bonduraunt School of Performance Driving—In The Racer's Seat." *Kit Car*. http://www.kitcarmag.com/eventcoverage/0807kc_bonduraunt_driving_school/photo_07.html.

Thompson, Neal. *Driving with the Devil*. New York: Crown Publishers, 2006.

Waid, Steve. "Earnhardt Wins Southeastern 500," In *The Earnhardt Collection: Because Winning Matters*. Chicago, IL: Triumph Books and Charlotte, NC: Street & Smith's Sports, 2006.

Willis, Ken. "Dale Was Destined for Greatness." *Racing News*. www.news-journalonline.com/speed/special/earnhardt/MEMMAIN.htm.

Wolfe, Tom. "The Last American Hero is Junior Johnson. Yes!" *Esquire*, 1965.

Woodford, Jennifer. "Dale Earnhardt: From the Pink K-2 to the Black #3." *All Race Magazine*, October 24, 2001. Revised July 12, 2002.

# FURTHER READING

Akers, Shawn A. "Dale Earnhardt's Daddy." *Concord-Kannapolis Independent Tribune*, May 17, 1997.

Auto Racing Daily. "Dale Jr. Talks About His Father, Career, and Marriage." http://www.autoracingdaily.com/news/latest-racing-news/dale-jr-talks about-his-father-career-and-marriage/.

AutoSpeak. "Dictionary of Racing Terms." http://www.autospeak.com/terms9 htm.

Baker, Andrew J. Roar: A Case Study of North Wilkesboro, NC and The Nor Wilkesboro Speedway 2005. http://www.savethespeedway.net/history html.

Barnett, Dave. "Where the Rubber Meets the Road—Establishing a Base Lin Vintage MG Club of Southern California. http://www.vintagemg.co ArticlePDFs/Tech107.pdf.

Bleacher Report. "NASCAR History: The Good Old Days, Pennsylvania Sty http://bleacherreport.com/articles/  27976-nascar-history-the-good-c days-pennsylvania-style.

Brooks, Marshall. Interview with the author. Concord, NC. October 16, 200

Burt, William. *The American Stock Car*. St Paul, MN: MBI Publishing, 2001.

Circle Track and Stock Car Magazine Editors. The Intimidator Dale Earnh: 23 Years with the Intimidator. St. Paul, MN: MBI Publishing, 2001.

Cothran, Larry and *Circle Track* and *Stock Car* Magazine Editors. *Earnh A Racing Family Legacy*. St. Paul, MN: Crestline (MBI), 2001.

*Dale*. DVD. Directed by Rory Karpf and Mike Viney. Charlotte, NC: NAS( Images and CMT Films, 2007.

Garner, Joe. *Speed, Guts and Glory*. New York: Warner Books, 2006.

# INDEX

## About the Author

GERRY SOUTER is a 30-year veteran photojournalist and author with more than 40 book titles to his credit from histories and biographies to Olympic sports and auto racing. He has covered Indianapolis 500-mile races and both open-wheel and touring races in Europe. His interests have included Formula One, Midgets, Drag Racing, and Sports Cars at Road America. He journeyed to North Carolina and "Earnhardt Country" to soak up the sights and sounds of NASCAR, see the places where the Earnhardts lived and walked, and talk with those who knew these racing legends.